The One-Stop History of the Bible

THE ONE-STOP
History of the Bible

Robert V. Huber and
Stephen M. Miller

LION

Published by Lion Books
an imprint of
Lion Hudson plc
Wilkinson House, Jordan Hill Road,
Oxford OX2 8DR, England
www.lionhudson.com/lion

ISBN 978 0 7459 7036 3
First published as *The Bible: A History* by Lion Hudson Plc, 2003

Acknowledgments
Unless otherwise marked Scripture quotations are from The New Revised Standard Version of
the Bible, copyright © 1989 by the Division of Christian Education of the National Council of
Churches in the USA. Used by permission. All Rights Reserved.
Extracts from The Authorized (King James) Version. Rights in the Authorized Version are vested
in the Crown. Reproduced by permission of the Crown's patentee, Cambridge University Press.
Excerpts from the New American Bible with Revised New Testament, are copyright © 1986,
1970 Confraternity of Christian Doctrine, Washington, D.C. and are used by permission of the
copyright owner. All rights reserved. No part of the New American Bible may be reproduced in
any form without permission in writing from the copyright owner.
Scripture quotations taken from the New American Standard Bible®, are copyright © 1960, 1962,
1963, 1968, 1971, 1972, 1973, 1975, 1977, 1995 by The Lockman Foundation. Used by permission.
Scripture quotations taken from the Holy Bible, New International Version, copyright © 1973,
1978, 1984 International Bible Society. Used by permission of Hodder & Stoughton, a member
of the Hodder Headline Group. All rights reserved. 'NIV' is a trademark of International Bible
Society. UK trademark number 1448790.
Scripture quotations taken from the Holy Bible, New Living Translation, copyright © 1996, 2004,
2007 by Tyndale House Foundation. Used by permission of Tyndale House Publishers, Inc., Carol
Stream, Illinois 60188. All rights reserved.
Scripture quotations marked *The Message* are taken from *The Message*. Copyright © by Eugene
H. Peterson 1993, 1994, 1995, 1996, 2000, 2001, 2002. Used by permission of NavPress Publishing
Group.

A catalogue record for this book is available from the British Library

Printed and bound in China, December 2015, LH06

Contents

Introduction

On the brink of execution, the apostle Paul wrote what many believe is his last surviving letter. He addressed it to his close friend Timothy, leader of a church in what is now Turkey. "All scripture is inspired by God," Paul wrote, "and is useful for teaching, for reproof, for correction, and for training in righteousness" (2 Timothy 3:16).

The jailed apostle was talking about Jewish Scripture, which Christians today call the Old Testament. Little did he know that one day Christians would consider his private letter part of sacred Scripture. Paul was probably no exception in this regard. As far as scholars can tell, none of the biblical writers knew their words would become part of the Holy Bible.

Yet, in time, people of faith came to recognize the word of God in these laws, history, poetry, wise sayings, prophecies, Gospels, and letters. How people came to this awareness remains a mystery. We do know that not all Jews agreed on which writings belonged in their Bible, and that Christians debated what to include in the New Testament. It was not until the late fourth century that the majority of church leaders ruled in favour of the collection of writings that make up the Bible today. Yet even now there is a bit of disagreement. Roman Catholics have an enlarged Old Testament, which includes several books and parts of books found in the Septuagint, the ancient Greek translation of Jewish Scripture. Eastern Orthodox churches add a few more.

No matter which of these collections is studied, there is astonishing consistency in the biblical books, though they were written by countless authors over a stretch of more than 1,000 years. The unifying element is God – his character and his continuing plan of salvation, a strategy for reaching out to people and saving them from sin and the harm it causes. Even though the Old and New Testaments were compiled by different theological camps of Jews and Christians, they unite to tell a seamless story of who God is and what he is doing to help humanity.

Why is the Bible so consistent when it comes to talking about God? And how has the Bible managed to survive for so many centuries? People of faith say that the answer lies with God himself. This is his story. It rests patiently on leather scrolls hidden in caves for 2,000 years. It outlasts flames kindled to silence it, and it fuels the passion of believers who make more copies. It survives critical study by sceptical scholars. It drives missionaries to take it to the ends of the earth. It even inspires translators to turn spoken languages into written languages for the sole purpose of letting others read God's story for themselves.

The One-Stop History of the Bible is not about the story of salvation that is told in the Bible. You can read that in Scripture itself. It is the story of the Bible – of how the Bible came to be, how it survived and how it changed the world throughout the centuries. It is a remarkable story.

Robert V. Huber and Stephen M. Miller

In the Beginning

FROM WORD OF MOUTH TO THE WRITTEN WORD

In the beginning there was no written word, only the spoken word. According to Genesis, the first book in the Bible, God created the universe and all it contains by speaking words. In turn, God's earliest worshippers used the spoken word to express their thoughts about their creator, and they passed this on by telling stories. Over time, several forms of writing were developed, and with the development of the Hebrew alphabet believers were able to write down their stories relating to God. These writings eventually became part of the Bible.

This cuneiform tablet from the seventh century BC was found at Nineveh. It contains lines from the Babylonian Epic of Gilgamesh, which tells a story of the Great Flood that parallels Genesis' account of Noah.

The Oral Tradition

At first, fathers and mothers probably told their children stories about their own parents and grandparents. Surely Abraham, the man God called to become the father of the nation that became Israel, must have told stories of how God called him to leave Ur and move to Canaan, promising he would be the father of a great nation. In doing so, Abraham would have preserved memories of his old life and used them to convince his neighbours in Canaan that the Lord was the one true God who had created the universe and performed other wondrous feats, such as saving Noah from the great flood. Abraham's son Isaac and his grandson Jacob would have continued the tradition, adding their own stories. In time, storytelling moved outside the family to professional storytellers, who performed at community gatherings. These stories continued to be repeated and passed on from generation to generation, preserving the culture of the people and letting them know who they were and how they differed from their neighbours. These retellings, now known as the oral tradition, were eventually written down.

More than Stories

Stories were not the only type of material passed on by storytellers. There were also proverbs, prayers, lyric poems, songs, laws, and even riddles (such as Samson's riddle in Judges 14:14) and aetiologies – stories that explain how some person or place got its name or how so many languages came into the world.

First Writings

While the Hebrews were passing on their culture by word of mouth, the world's first writing systems were being put to use in Mesopotamia and Egypt. A system of chiselling symbols into stone or adding them to clay tablets evolved in Mesopotamia in about 3200 BC. This was called cuneiform. Most often, the symbols were cut into wet clay tablets using a stylus with a wedge-shaped tip. The tablets were then left to dry and then baked in a kiln to harden them. The earliest symbols were rough pictograms, but they became more and more abstract as time went on. The Egyptians developed their own writing system, either soon after or a bit before the appearance of cuneiform. In Egypt, writing was in the form of hieroglyphics: pictographs that were usually done with pen and ink on papyrus, but were also painted on the walls of palaces, temples, and tombs.

Below is a Mesopotamian administrative seal in the form of a clay cuneiform tablet dating from between 3100 and 2900 BC. The earliest cuneiform symbols were crude pictographs, which could be combined to denote actions or ideas. Over time, the symbols grew ever more abstract.

We have heard with our ears, O God, our ancestors have told us, what deeds you performed in their days, in the days of old.
PSALM 44:1

Writing Hebrew

Because both cuneiform and hieroglyphics utilized thousands of symbols, only highly trained scribes could read and write. In the late Bronze Age (1525–1200 BC), writing was made simpler with the development of alphabets. Although the earliest surviving alphabet was created before the Phoenicians arrived in Canaan (about 1200 BC), the Phoenicians produced the most extensive body of surviving texts using an alphabet between 1050 and 850 BC. Consequently the ancient Canaanite alphabet is known as the Phoenician. The Hebrew alphabet is a direct descendant. After settling in their Promised Land in Canaan, the Hebrews adapted the Phoenician alphabet to their own language. Like English, Hebrew is written horizontally across a page, but unlike English it is written from right to left. The Hebrew alphabet consists of 22 consonants. The vowel sounds are omitted in written Hebrew and must be supplied by the reader. This requires choices. For example, if we wrote English in the Hebrew way, the written word "ntcv" would have to be reversed to read from left to right as "vctn" and vowels supplied, which, depending on context, could give us either "vocation" or "vacation".

Keeping the Language Constant

Except for a few scattered chapters and verses, all the books of the Old Testament are written in Hebrew. But even though these books were written over a period of nearly 1,000 years – and incorporated even older, oral traditions – there is strikingly little difference between the oldest texts and the newest. This is astounding, as most languages change constantly. For example, English literature of 1,000 years ago is totally unreadable today by someone with no special training. Not so the Old Testament. The reason for the consistency of Hebrew writing may be that the texts of Scripture were so revered that they had a profound effect on the language itself, keeping it constant.

This Egyptian funerary stele features hieroglyphic writing with a depiction of a married couple.

THE ART OF THE STORYTELLER

Storytellers thrived in most ancient cultures, and their stories often paralleled each other. For example, Babylonian storytellers told how the heavens and earth were created by a group of battling gods, while the Bible claims that one God created everything. Because they drew large repeat crowds, storytellers in all traditions often embellished or combined tales to keep them vibrant. However, if a storyteller altered a story's essential truths, listeners who had heard the stories before would haughtily correct them.

Moses Gives the Law

WRITTEN IN STONE, THEN ON PAPYRUS

Moses, the leader of the Israelites' exodus from Egypt, gave his people the hundreds of laws preserved in the first five books of the Bible. At first, God had personally laid down his laws in a speech before the entire nation, punctuating them with thunder and lightning. However, the experience was so frightening that the people pleaded with Moses to serve as intermediary between them and God. Moses agreed, then climbed Mount Sinai, where he received God's laws. The most important – the Ten Commandments – were engraved on two stone tablets. Later these and other laws would be transcribed onto papyrus scrolls.

Laws That Define a Nation

The Ten Commandments became the fundamental laws of Judaism, on which all other Jewish laws are based. Many of the more than 600 subsequent laws handed down by Moses (the Mosaic law) probably came to the prophet while the Israelites were still camped at Mount Sinai. They are of two types. Some, like the Ten Commandments, set down broad principles that help people remain in harmony with one another and faithful to God. Others apply to specific cases; for example: "When someone steals an ox… the thief shall pay five oxen" (Exodus 22:1).

Some of the Mosaic laws are so distinctive they actually define the nation. Israelites could be recognized by the way they looked and behaved. As the law required, Israelites did not eat certain foods, such as pork, they did not work on the Sabbath (Saturdays), and Israelite males were circumcised.

Other law codes in the Middle East covered only secular matters, such as setting penalties for stealing and outlining procedures for getting a divorce. But Mosaic law covered both secular and religious matters, demonstrating that God ruled both domains. Other law codes also operated on the basis of class distinction, with the upper classes drawing milder penalties than commoners. Under Mosaic law, aristocrats and commoners were treated alike, and people were mandated to protect the helpless, especially widows and orphans.

Other Laws in Stone

The Ten Commandments were not the first laws to be etched in stone. Much earlier, in the eighteenth century BC, a Babylonian king, Hammurabi, had 282 laws inscribed onto a black stone pillar (right). At the top of the stone Hammurabi is shown receiving laws from the sun god Shamash. The laws are inscribed below the image.

Left: Moses smashes the tablets of the Law in this 1659 painting by Rembrandt.

PAPYRUS: PAPER FROM THE NILE

Made from tall slender reeds that grew in dense clusters along the Nile and other waterways, papyrus was the world's first lightweight, inexpensive, and durable writing material. From about 3000 BC, Egyptian craftsmen cut the stems into sections, then cut away the outside layer of the stem, exposing the soft cylinder of white pith inside. They then sliced the moist pith into thin strips, dried the strips, and worked them into sheets. To make a sheet, a craftsman laid a number of strips side by side, then added a second row on top, with its strips running crossways to the first layer. The craftsman then hammered and pressed the strips until the pith fibres intertwined, binding the two layers. When dried in the sun, the sheets presented a strong, flexible, creamy white writing surface. Scribes could write on individual papyrus sheets or glue several end to end with flour paste to form a scroll. The Bible itself owes its name to papyrus. Greeks called papyrus rolls *biblia*, after Phoenicia's seaport of Byblos, a major exporter of papyrus. In time, the word came to mean "book" and eventually "the Book", the Bible.

Two figures and hieroglyphics decorate a sheet of papyrus. Holding the sheet up to the light reveals that it is constructed by laying strips of papyrus stems at right angles to each other.

Pens and Ink
Early scribes wrote on papyrus with small brush-like pens cut from rushes, tiny plants that grew in the marsh, or reeds sharpened to a point and split like a quill pen. Pens were often kept in wooden boxes, as shown here.

The Oral Law

Jewish tradition says that many of the laws and explanations that God gave Moses were not written, but were passed along by word of mouth. The oral law, as it became known, included supplemental laws and guidance that reinforced the written law. For instance, the written law said to honour the Sabbath by not working. The oral law defined what was and was not work. As times changed, religious leaders adjusted and expanded these oral laws to adapt to the times. These oral laws were carried on strictly by word of mouth until about AD 200, when they were finally written down. This is called the Mishnah.

The Nature of Moses' Stone Tablets

The Bible says little about what the Ten Commandments looked like, except that they were written on both sides of two stone tablets (Exodus 32:15). They probably were not as large as those shown in paintings and films, otherwise Moses would have had a hard time carrying them down Mount Sinai. Some scholars suggest the tablets may have been slabs of limestone, a relatively light rock, which, like shale, can be broken into thin slabs. People throughout the Middle East often wrote on such slabs.

Papyrus stalks, which grew along river banks, as seen here, were transformed into a forerunner of today's paper.

David and His Royal Writers

EARLY ISRAELITE PROSE AND POETRY

The Bible relates many colourful and dramatic stories about David, Israel's greatest king. They tell how the shepherd boy David, who sometimes played the lyre and sang to soothe Israel's first king, Saul, killed the giant Goliath with a sling shot, then went on to become Israel's next king and greatly expand Saul's kingdom. But perhaps David's biggest contribution was that he started the almost millennium-long process of writing the Bible. Although writing in Hebrew was very new in David's time, as king, he commissioned a history of the emerging nation he led and probably encouraged the writing down of the histories, laws, poems, and songs that were being passed along as part of the oral tradition. David also wrote songs and psalms of his own.

Recording Israel's Culture and History

By about 1000 BC, having secured Israel's borders, King David set up his royal cabinet, which included two writers: "Jehoshaphat son of Ahilud was the recorder; Sheva was secretary" (2 Samuel 20:24–25). It is likely that the secretary saw to David's correspondence, while the recorder supervised the writing down and circulating of the king's decrees. The recorder may also have overseen a group of scribes who were commissioned to write down and preserve Israel's well-known stories and laws and to chronicle the events of David's reign – and later the reigns of his successors.

These chronicles, or annals, served a political purpose for David, as well as preserving the history of Israel. Because it was expected that a king's oldest surviving son should inherit his father's throne, and David was not related at all to Saul, the previous king, questions had been raised about the legitimacy of David's reign. The annals offered compelling evidence that David was, indeed, blessed of God, thus legitimizing the rule of David and his successors. Future kings continued the practice of keeping annals of their reigns.

BIBLICAL POETRY

Almost every book of the Old Testament contains at least some poetry. Several books have nothing but poetry, including Psalms, Proverbs, the Song of Solomon, and Lamentations. The oracles proclaimed by the Prophets and the book of Job are largely in poetic form.

Unlike English verse, biblical poetry is not characterized by rhyme or regular rhythm. Instead it often relies on parallelism. There are three basic forms of parallelism. In the first, called synonymous parallelism, an idea expressed in one half of a verse is echoed in different words in the second:

Let justice roll down like waters.
And righteousness like an ever-flowing stream.
Amos 5:24

In the second type of parallelism, antithetical, opposite statements are made in the two halves of the verse:

The Lord watches over the way of the righteous,
But the way of the wicked will perish.
Psalm 1:6

In the third type of parallelism, constructive, or synthetic, the ideas neither repeat nor contradict. Instead, the second half of a verse line builds on the first half:

Like a gold ring in a pig's snout
is a beautiful woman without good sense.
Proverbs 11:22

In addition to parallelism, Hebrew poetry uses many of the devices of English poetry, including alliteration and the repetition of words and phrases. Some poems are acrostic, or alphabetic, with each verse beginning with the next letter of the Hebrew alphabet.

Is this not written in the Book of Jashar? The sun stopped in midheaven, and did not hurry to set for about a whole day.

JOSHUA 10:13B

SEE ALSO
THE PSALMS, PP. 14–15
UNFLATTERING HISTORY, PP. 20–21

The Annals and Other Lost Books as Source Material

Although all of the ancient annals have been lost, they are often referred to in the biblical books of Samuel, Kings, and Chronicles, which had obviously used them as sources. Typically, the discussion of a king's reign in the Bible ends with a referral to one of these annals, such as: "Now, the rest of the acts of Ahab, and all that he did, and the ivory house that he built, and all the cities that he built, are they not written in the Book of the Annals of the kings of Israel?" (1 Kings 22:39).

The annals are not the only lost books to be referred to in the Old Testament. In fact, 23 titles are referred to, though scholars estimate that there were only some half a dozen actual books, some of which are cited under multiple titles. In addition to various annals of the kings of Judah and Israel there are histories of various prophets and two collections of ancient poems: *The Book of the Wars of the Lord* (cited in Numbers 21:14) contains a poem in Hebrew that is so old it is hard to translate. The *Book of Jashar* contains at least two ancient poems: Joshua's prayer asking that the sun stand still (Joshua 10:12–13) and David's lament on the deaths of Saul and Jonathan (2 Samuel 1:17–27).

Above: During the Battle of Gibeon, shown here in an illustration from an early fifteenth-century Spanish Bible, Joshua prays that the sun would stand still to give his men time to defeat their enemy. The prayer had first appeared in the *Book of Jashar*.

Below: After passing through the miraculously parted waters of the Red Sea, Moses' sister Miriam led the Israelite women in a song, as depicted in this painting by Simeon Solomon. Miriam's song (Exodus 15:20–21) and the Song of Deborah (Judges 5:1–31) are considered to be among the oldest texts in the Bible.

Opposite: David defeats Goliath, as depicted in a nineteenth-century stained glass at St Aignan Church, Chartres.

Jewish Worship and the Psalms

REACHING OUT TO GOD IN SONG

When the Israelites started worshipping God during their years in the wilderness, they had neither sacred scriptures to use in prayer nor a place to worship. Then God gave Moses the Ten Commandments and other laws. Some of these laws instructed the people to build a tent worship centre, called the tabernacle. Others told them when and how to offer sacrifices – the principal method of worship at the time. When the people put these laws into practice, they accompanied their processions and rites of sacrifice with prayerful songs, or psalms.

Below: Jewish men meet in the synagogue to study Scripture and ancient commentaries by revered Jewish teachers. Reading the Bible is a key part of Jewish worship.

Worship at the Temple

By the time the temple was built in Jerusalem, replacing the earlier tabernacle tent, early versions of biblical texts had been committed to writing and the Israelites used these Scriptures in worship. Often they proclaimed them or made references to their contents. For example, Deuteronomy 26:3–11 mandates that worshippers who bring offerings to the temple from the early harvest should present the offering to the priest, refer to the mighty acts God had performed to bring the Israelites into the Promised Land, as related in the Scriptures, and then declare, "So now I bring the first of the fruit of the ground that you, O Lord, have given me."

Lots of music accompanied temple rites. King David, a psalmist himself, organized religious choirs and appointed a musician to direct them in song, accompanied by harps, lyres, trumpets, and cymbals – the word "psalm" is from the Greek *psalmos*, meaning the "twanging of strings". Music echoed from the Jerusalem hilltop as priests offered the morning and evening sacrifices and as worshippers brought their offerings. Some worshippers arrived singing Songs of Ascent (Psalms 120–134), so called because people approached the temple by climbing the hill upon which it was built. There were also special songs for weddings and coronations, recaps of Israel's history, and, most plentiful of all, psalms of lament – poignant expressions of sorrow or fear over the treachery of friends, the threats of enemies, sickness, loneliness, or the sense of being forsaken by God.

Above: Flute made from bone, which was excavated in Jerusalem, the city of David.

Worship in the Synagogue

After the Jews had been exiled to Babylon, they had no place to worship. The Jerusalem temple was in ruins, and far away. Scholars suspect that it was during this exile that synagogues emerged as substitutes for the temple. The word "synagogue" comes from the Greek for "assembly". Unlike the temple, synagogues were not run by priests, nor could people offer sacrifices there – Mosaic law permitted sacrifices only at the temple. But the synagogue was where Jews stayed in touch with their sacred teachings and traditions.

SINGERS' GUILDS

Some psalms are attributed to singers' guilds, either the Sons of Korah or the Sons of Asaph. Occasionally, a psalm is attributed to an individual member of one of these guilds. Psalm 88, for example, is attributed to Heman of the Sons of Korah. As the names suggest, each guild was made up of members of a family, whose job was to sing at worship services.

It is not clear whether the guild members composed psalms or merely preserved and performed them. They probably did all of the above in addition to revising older psalms to fit new circumstances, as some psalms are repeated with only minor changes. For example, Psalm 40:13–17 repeats Psalm 70, following a section of 12 other verses.

Make a joyful noise to the Lord, all the earth,
Worship the Lord with gladness; come into his presence with singing.
PSALM 100:1–2

THE BOOK OF PSALMS

The book of Psalms, which is often described as the temple's hymnbook, is made up of 150 psalms. Many of them are attributed to individuals in superscriptions or subtitles – probably added long after the psalms were composed. Almost half the psalms are attributed to King David, though many of these were probably not actually written by David, but simply invoke his spirit.

No one knows when the psalms were written, but they seem to span nearly a millennium, from the exodus through to the Babylonian exile. Psalm 90 is attributed to Moses and may have been written by him, though it could well have been written later as a prayer in the spirit of Moses. Psalm 137 was certainly written after the exile, as it looks back in time to the exile: "By the rivers of Babylon – there we sat down and there we wept when we remembered Zion" (Psalm 137:1).

The individual psalms were probably used in public and private worship long before they were collected into a single volume. How and when the songs were compiled remains a mystery and may have taken place over several centuries – with new songs being added after they gradually became an established part of Jewish worship tradition. The final compilation took place sometime after the Babylonian exile. Today both Christians and Jews continue to use the psalms to express their deepest feelings to God.

King David playing a psaltery.

Typically, a synagogue service included readings from the law of Moses (the first five books of the Bible) and from other books of the Hebrew Bible. There were also prayers and a sermon. Visitors were often invited to read from the sacred scrolls and address the worshippers. It was in a synagogue that Jesus read a passage from Isaiah, which predicted the coming era of the Messiah, and then declared the prophecy fulfilled (Luke 4:21). The apostle Paul later took advantage of the visitor-friendly custom by telling assembled Jews about Jesus.

After the Romans destroyed the Jewish temple in AD 70, it was never rebuilt, and Jews could no longer sacrifice animals or make crop offerings. Instead, they continued to meet in synagogues to pray, reflect on Scripture, and sing psalms.

This Egyptian wall painting from the tomb of Rekhmere (a court official) shows female musicians with a harp and other stringed instruments.

Shaping the Pentateuch

TRANSFORMING ORAL TRADITIONS INTO WRITING

Although much was written down during the time of King David, accounts of the origins of the Israelites and their beliefs continued to be circulated by word of mouth. These accounts were eventually preserved in written form in the books of Genesis, Exodus, Leviticus, Numbers, and Deuteronomy – the first five books of the Bible, known as the Pentateuch (from the Greek for "five-book work"). Because it was long believed that Moses had written it, the Pentateuch was generally referred to as the Five Books of Moses. Today, however, scholars believe that the Pentateuch was assembled by numerous authors well after the time of Moses.

Questioning Moses' Authorship

Through the centuries scholars fostered doubts that Moses had single-handedly written the Pentateuch. They pointed out conflicting dates and place names and noted that some of the events depicted had occurred after the time of Moses – including Moses' death and burial. More importantly, they found many doublets (two versions of a single story). For example, in Genesis 1:27 God creates man and woman together; in Genesis 2:21–22, he creates a woman out of the man's rib. Similarly, in Genesis 7:2–3, Noah takes aboard the ark seven pairs of each kind of ritually clean animal but only one pair of each unclean animal. In Genesis 6:19–20 and 7:8–9, he takes aboard only one pair of each species, whether clean or unclean.

Some early scholars concluded that Moses had written the Pentateuch, but that later scribes had added material to it. A few claimed that the Pentateuch was written by Ezra, the priest and scribe who instituted religious reform in Jerusalem after the Babylonian exile.

Four Sources

In more recent times close study of doublets led to an important theory. Scholars noticed that one part of a doublet used the name Yahweh for God while the other used the word Elohim, the Hebrew word meaning "god". This suggested that at least two traditions were interwoven in the Pentateuch. Later scholars found more. In 1878 the German scholar Julius Wellhausen studied all the viable theories and proposed a schema called the Documentary Hypothesis.

Wellhausen saw four basic sources: J, E, P, and D. He named the first two for the words they used for God: J stands for Jahveh (German for Yahweh) and E stands for Elohim. He called the third source P, for priestly, because it focuses on priests. D stands for the book of Deuteronomy, which makes up the fourth source. These sources had been written as separate accounts at different times, in different places, and by different people and were combined in stages. They themselves incorporated even earlier sources.

According to Genesis, Noah took aboard either seven pairs of each clean animal or one pair of each species.

HOW THE SOURCES DIFFER

Although today some scholars are critical of the Documentary Hypothesis and offer their own versions of it, others continue to accept Wellhausen's model, which holds the following:

- **J** probably dates to ninth-century BC Judah – after the northern tribes had split away to form the kingdom of Israel. J's literary style is lively and colourful. It stresses the monarchy and stories and traditions of the southern tribes, including those of Abraham.

- **E**, which probably dates to the eighth century, focuses on the leadership of Moses and the prophets rather than kings. Its style is more sophisticated than J's and God is less personal. E stresses traditions from the northern kingdom. In the mid seventh century after the fall of the northern kingdom, E was combined with J.

- **D**, or at least a large part of it, probably made up the book of law that was found in the temple in 621 BC and read to the reformer King Josiah (2 Kings 22:8). It emphasizes the need for central worship, as advocated by Josiah. D was probably added to the combined J and E in the mid sixth century.

- **P** may have been added to the earlier sources during or just after the Babylonian exile by priests who were attempting to preserve the origins of temple rituals. In P the priest is the ultimate authority; prophets play no part. P is more rigid in tone than J or E and is concerned with ages and dates not found elsewhere, as in its account of the Flood (Genesis 7:11 and 8:4–5).

Joseph is sold into slavery to either Ishmaelite or Midianite traders.

Closely Knit Texts

The editors of the Pentateuch, whoever they were, did a masterful job of pulling the texts together. In some cases, they simply placed stories from different sources one after the other, as in the two versions of the creation. Elsewhere, as in the story of Joseph, they knit E and J sources together so tightly it is hard to separate them. For example, Genesis 37:21–24 reports that Reuben keeps his brothers from murdering Joseph by convincing them to throw him into a pit. He is planning to rescue Joseph later, but before he can, the other brothers sell Joseph into slavery to a group of Midianites. But Genesis 37:25–27 says that it is Judah who saves Joseph's life, suggesting that he be sold to a band of Ishmaelites. Then these two traditions come together in a single verse that names both Midianites and Ishmaelites: "When some Midianite traders passed by, they drew Joseph up, lifting him out of the pit, and sold him to the Ishmaelites" (Genesis 37:28). This passage also demonstrates the northern and southern biases of E and J: in E Reuben, whose descendants settled in the north, saves Joseph, while in J Judah, whose descendants settled in the south, does so.

The editors also linked together strains of the various sources by adding genealogies or even single words – such as "again" to justify repetitions. The editors always took care, however, never to significantly change or delete material from their sources, which they held sacred.

THAT'S ANOTHER STORY

In chapter 14 of 2 Esdras, one of the books of the Apocrypha (books that did not quite make it into the Old Testament), God tells Ezra to assemble five scribes and to dictate to them what God will inspire him to say. Ezra dictates for 40 days, and his scribes copy down the 24 books of the Old Testament plus 70 other sacred books. In this text, now generally regarded as myth, Ezra, not Moses, is seen as the author of the Pentateuch.

Prophets and Scribes

BRINGING THE WORD OF GOD TO THE PEOPLE

In the early days of their history, the Israelites had no king. Or rather, God was their king, and he kept in touch with his people through prophets – men and women who spoke for him.

In the 200 years or so after the Israelites settled in the Promised Land, prophets advised the judges who ruled the land. Some, notably Deborah, served as both prophet and judge. The last judge–prophet was Samuel, who anointed Israel's first two kings, Saul and David. But even in the days of the kings, prophets wielded power, advising the people and their leaders and even boldly confronting kings who disregarded God's will. Stories of the early prophets – along with some of their prophecies – are found in the books of Joshua, Judges, Samuel, and Kings. In the Jewish Bible these books are known as the Former Prophets. The words of 15 Later Prophets, sometimes called the writing prophets, are recorded in biblical books that bear their names.

Scribes generally closed their scrolls with tiny chunks of clay, called *bullae*, into which they impressed their seals. The *bulla* shown here is inscribed in Ancient Hebrew: "To Hezekiah (son of) Ahaz, King (of) Judah", the subject of 2 Kings 18–20.

Above: The north rose window of Chartres Cathedral illustrates Old Testament prophets (in circles) and kings (in squares).

Then Jeremiah called Baruch son of Neriah, and Baruch wrote on a scroll at Jeremiah's dictation all the words of the Lord that he had spoken to him.

JEREMIAH 36:4

● SEE ALSO
SETTLING THE JEWISH BIBLE,
PP. 26–27

JONAH

The book of Jonah is unique among the prophetic books in that it is mainly a story of a reluctant prophet sent by God to convert Israel's enemies, the Ninevites. Its only prophecy is: "Forty days more and Nineveh will be destroyed" (Jonah 3:4). It was written in the fifth or fourth century BC to teach the Israelites to love even their enemies.

Sculpture of the prophet Jeremiah at Moissac Abbey Church in France.

The Writing Prophets

The earliest writing prophets were Hosea and Amos, who called for reforms in the northern kingdom of Israel. (After Solomon's death his kingdom had split into two kingdoms.) Hosea and Amos assured the people that the Lord would protect them if they turned back to him, stopped worshipping idols, and cared for the needy. Similarly, the prophets Micah and Isaiah condemned the injustices and idolatry they found in both Israel and the southern kingdom of Judah. Isaiah also warned that God would send the Assyrians to invade Israel as punishment for the sins of the people. All these prophets went unheeded and, as Isaiah had foreseen, the Assyrians obliterated the northern kingdom of Israel. After 721 BC it no longer existed.

Later prophets turned their attention to the surviving kingdom of Judah, generally begging the people to remember the Lord and follow his word. They included Zephaniah, Nahum, Habakkuk, and the unstoppable Jeremiah, who advised Judah's last five kings.

In 597 BC the Babylonians invaded Jerusalem and sent 8,000 Jews, including Ezekiel, into exile in Babylon. From exile Ezekiel prophesied the destruction of Jerusalem's temple, but his people ignored him. When the Babylonians invaded Jerusalem again in 586 BC and did destroy the temple, Ezekiel preached hope: God would resurrect Israel, like a pile of dry bones coming back to life. In 539 BC Babylonia was conquered by Cyrus the Great of Persia, who freed the exiles.

Last Prophetic Writings

The book of Isaiah had predicted Cyrus's release of the exiles in chapters 40–55, which were probably written by an anonymous prophet using the name of the earlier prophet Isaiah. Later, from Jerusalem, either the same prophet – called Second Isaiah – or a different one wrote the passages contained in Isaiah 56–66. This "Third Isaiah" encouraged the Israelites to rebuild Jerusalem, predicting that God's salvation would come not to Judah alone, but to all the world.

In addition, five other prophets made their voices heard in post-exilic times – each with a biblical book of his own. Obadiah condemned the Edomites, a neighbouring people, for not having helped the Israelites when the Babylonians had invaded and taken them into exile. Haggai and Zechariah urged the returning Israelites to rebuild the temple. A little later, Joel described a plague of locusts as a punishment from God and urged repentance, and Malachi told the people that God loved them and pointed to the coming of the Messiah.

SETTING IT DOWN

Generally, prophets delivered their prophecies spontaneously, perhaps accompanied by music and dancing. But their words were later written down in highly structured poetic form, and no one knows by whom. The prophets themselves may have later written down and polished their own pronouncements, or disciples of the prophets may have done so, editing them to fit new circumstances. In some cases, they probably even added to the prophecies. The book of Isaiah suggests this process, as its writings cover a period of some 200 years – too long for one man to have prophesied.

Prophetic works were also preserved by scribes, as vividly described in chapter 36 of Jeremiah. We read there that when King Jehoiakim of Judah forbade Jeremiah to proclaim his prophecies, God told the prophet to write down all his words and have them read to the king. Jeremiah then dictated all his past prophecies to his scribe, Baruch, who copied them down in a scroll. Baruch then went to the temple, where he publicly read Jeremiah's words. Officials of the king took the scroll and read it to the king, who then burned the scroll. But the prophecies were not lost, for Jeremiah again dictated his prophecies to Baruch. The new scroll probably formed the basis for the first 25 chapters of the book of Jeremiah.

Israel's Unflattering History

SPECULATING ON WHAT WENT WRONG

In 586 BC the Babylonians attacked Jerusalem, levelling the temple and dragging survivors off to exile in Babylon. Bereft of everything, the exiles wondered how this could have happened. Some searched for answers in their history, compiling and editing the stories and teachings of their ancestors. Because the compilers were truly searching for the causes of their predicament, they preserved all that seemed relevant, good or bad. Several thoughtful revisions transformed this unflattering history into the biblical books of Joshua, Judges, 1 and 2 Samuel, and 1 and 2 Kings.

King David watches the beautiful Bathsheba bathe, leading him into adultery and murder. This story was included in the Bible to show the type of sinfulness that led to Judah's fall.

The Deuteronomists

Although the Bible's historical books were completed during or just after the Babylonian exile, scholars believe that they were compiled and reshaped over a period of time by the same writers/editors who had produced the book of Deuteronomy, which seems to form an introduction to the series and share its literary style. Consequently, the authors of these books are often called the Deuteronomists. They were probably the descendants of the priests Jeroboam had ousted.

Reasons Behind the Horror

During the exodus, the Israelites had entered a covenant, or contract, with God whereby if they devoted themselves to him and his laws, God would give them land, prosperity, and protection. If they broke the covenant, they would lose everything. God kept the covenant, but the Israelites did not. They repeatedly turned away from God, returning only when they got into trouble – or when God sent corrective punishment. After the wise King Solomon fell into idolatry, his kingdom was split in two: Israel in the north and Judah in the south.

Jeroboam, the first king of the northern kingdom, fostered idolatry and appointed priests from among the people instead of using priests from the tribe of Levi as Mosaic law required. The legitimate priests Jeroboam had ousted joined together to preserve their beliefs and moved to Jerusalem.

As the Israelites and their kings continued to sin and practise idolatry, God sent prophets to warn them about what would happen if they did not repent. They did not listen, and in 722 BC Assyrian invaders decimated the northern kingdom of Israel. However, the people of Judah failed to see the connection between sin and judgment in Israel, and in 586 BC they suffered a similar fate at the hands of Babylonians.

Jeroboam's Idolatry by Jean-Honoré Fragonard (1732–1806).

> *By the waters of Babylon – there we sat down and there we wept when we remembered Zion [Jerusalem].*
>
> PSALM 137:1

EVIDENCE FROM OUTSIDE THE BIBLE

Cynics often dismiss the Old Testament histories as pious fictions. Archaeologists, however, have found non-Jewish inscriptions that authenticate them. A few follow:

- About 1210 BC, Pharaoh Merneptah of Egypt had inscribed on a black slab that due to his military campaigns in Canaan, "Israel is laid waste". This is the earliest mention of Israel outside the Bible.

- In 840–820 BC, on a monument known as the Moabite Stone, King Mesha of Moab claimed to have "utterly destroyed forever" the descendants of "Omri, king of Israel", though three of Omri's descendants went on to rule Israel.

- In 841 BC, on a black marble obelisk, Israel's King Jehu is pictured bowing down to Assyria's King Shalmaneser III above a list of the tribute of gold and silver paid by Jehu.

- During the ninth century BC, a commemorative stone celebrating an Aramean victory over the Israelites used the words "Beit David" ("House of David"). Before this stone was discovered in 1993 sceptics had claimed that David was mythical. This inscription, plus others found later, proved otherwise.

- In 701 BC, on a six-sided clay cylinder, Assyria's King Sennacherib tells how he invaded Judah and besieged Jerusalem, shutting up Israel's King Hezekiah "like a caged bird".

- In 539 BC, when Cyrus the Great overpowered Babylon and started the Persian Empire, he issued a decree – inscribed on a clay cylinder – that freed all prisoners of the Babylonian Empire, including the exiled Jews.

Left: The Cylinder of Cyrus, dating from 539 BC, which tells of the decree recorded in the book of Ezra permitting the Jews who were exiles in Babylon to go to Judah and rebuild the temple.

Above: The first mention of the name of Israel is on this stone slab found at Thebes, which records the military triumph of Pharaoh Merneptah.

The First Edition

Some time after the northern kingdom of Israel fell to the Assyrians the Deuteronomists compiled a history to explain why. However, the Deuteronomists' texts were not histories as such, but theological commentaries on history. Each king was judged only on his relationship with God. If a king allowed pagan worship, he was evil. If he maintained God's law, he was good. Most of the kings of Israel had been evil, and so Israel fell, but Judah's current king, Josiah, was good and under his rule Judah would prosper with God offering full support.

A Revised Edition

The optimism of the Deuteronomists was dashed when Josiah was killed in battle and the next four kings were not good ones. When Jerusalem fell, there were no more kings. The Deuteronomists reworked their history, insisting that it was not merely the kings who had done wrong, but the people as a whole. The revised edition made it clear that God had established his covenant with the people themselves and not merely their rulers. God remained faithful to his covenant even though the people repeatedly failed to do so. But when trouble came and the people repented, God always forgave them. Perhaps, the history suggests, if the exiles turn back to God, he will forgive them again and restore them to his favour. After the exile ended the revised text was joined to the Pentateuch.

The Writings

The Jewish Bible is divided into three parts: Law (the Pentateuch), Prophets (stories and words of the prophets), and Writings. The Writings contain the Psalms and 10 books of teachings and stories devoted to helping people live good lives. These books can be roughly divided into wisdom, history, and pseudo-historical books. The Writings were probably the last books to be added to the Jewish Bible, but not all of them were among the last to be written. Parts of Psalms, Proverbs, and Job may be nearly as old as the law. However, most of the books were written after the end of the Babylonian exile.

Job is in pain, and his wife urges him to curse God. Job's story may be one of the oldest in the Bible. A similar tale, referred to as the Sumerian Job, dates from before 2000 BC.

Wisdom Literature

Wisdom literature is the label given to writings that teach readers how to lead a good life. Proverbs, Job, and Ecclesiastes are the main wisdom books, but sometimes Song of Solomon and selected psalms are included.

- The book of Proverbs is a collection of short verse sayings, often assembled in groups. Basically they hold that wisdom, founded on respect for God, is needed to succeed in life – materially, physically, socially, and morally. The sayings were written by many sages over a period of centuries.

- Job and Ecclesiastes were written to question the idea found repeatedly in Proverbs – and some psalms – that good people are always rewarded while evildoers are always punished. Job recounts the ancient story of a righteous man who loses everything. When friends insist that he must have done something to deserve punishment, Job insists on his innocence and asks God why he must suffer so. In the end, God speaks, asking Job if he had been present at the creation and letting us know that we cannot understand the ways of God, who is so far above humanity in everything. Ecclesiastes is an even darker reflection on the problem of evil in the world. Holding that all of life is vanity, the author nevertheless maintains his love of God.

- The Song of Solomon – a passionate love poem – demonstrates how a man and a woman should love one another. Although the poem seems totally secular, it has long been interpreted as an allegory of God's love for Israel or Christ's love for his church. The author is unknown, but the poem is sometimes attributed to Solomon, who appears briefly and who is known for his great wisdom.

Historical Books

After the exile some Jews, including Daniel and Esther, chose to remain in Babylon under the new Persian ruler, while others returned home. Among the later returnees were Ezra, a priest and scribe, and Nehemiah, who, as governor of Judah, saw to the rebuilding of Jerusalem's walls. Several new histories were written at that time.

- The books 1 and 2 Chronicles (originally a single book), retrace the history of the Israelites to the end of the Babylonian exile. In so doing, they present David and Solomon as ideal rulers, omitting their blemishes (such as David's adultery), and pay only scant – and generally negative – attention to the northern kingdom of Israel.

- Ezra and Nehemiah, which also began as a single book, tell of the Jews returning to Jerusalem after the exile to rebuild the temple and the city itself. Scholars believe that the priest Ezra may have been the author of Chronicles and Ezra and Nehemiah.

- The book of Daniel relates stories of the religious persecution of Daniel and his Jewish friends at the end of Babylonian times and the beginning of the Persian Empire. The stories were probably not compiled, however, until the time of the Maccabean revolt in 167 BC, when a Seleucid (Syrian) king tried to wipe out the Jewish religion. The book is often seen as a book of prophecy because of the predictions Daniel makes.

The fear of the Lord is the beginning of knowledge; fools despise wisdom and instruction.

PROVERBS 1:7

● SEE ALSO
THE PSALMS, PP. 14–15
UNFLATTERING HISTORY, PP. 20–21
SETTLING THE JEWISH BIBLE, PP. 26–27

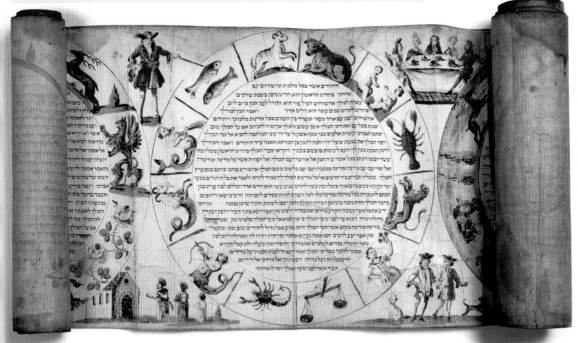

The "Esther scroll" is used on the joyous feast of Purim, when the story of Esther is read to celebrate deliverance from a Persian holocaust.

Pseudo-Historical Books

The remaining books of the Writings touch more lightly on history.

■ The tender story of Ruth – David's non-Jewish great-grandmother – may have been written in David's time, but it was probably not finalized until the time of Ezra. If so, Ruth's story would have provided a compelling argument against Ezra's command that Jewish men divorce their non-Jewish wives. For it is clear that God selected Ruth, a non-Jew, to found the royal line of David.

■ Lamentations is a series of five elegies that lament the fall of Jerusalem and call upon Jews to repent their sins and hope in God. The prophet Jeremiah was long thought to have written these poems, but his authorship has been questioned.

■ The book of Esther tells of a beautiful Jewish girl who becomes queen of Persia, the empire that defeated the Babylonians, and saves the Persian Jews from a holocaust.

EZRA, THE SECOND LAWGIVER

The scribe Ezra was given a commission by King Artaxerxes of Persia to return to Jerusalem and teach the people the law of Moses. When he arrived, Ezra discovered that many Jewish men had pagan wives, so he insisted that they divorce these idol worshippers. Then he read from the book of Moses (the Pentateuch). The people were enthralled. From that time to this the law of Moses has been the focal point of Jewish worship. Moses had been the Jewish people's first lawgiver. Ezra, by restoring the Mosaic law, is considered their second lawgiver.

Ezra the Scribe, in an illustration from a seventh- or eighth-century manuscript from Italy.

First Translations of the Bible

SCRIPTURE IN UPDATED LANGUAGES

By the time the Israelites had returned from exile in Babylon, they had lost touch with much of their heritage – including their ancestral language. Instead of Hebrew, most Jews spoke only Aramaic, the language of the Persian Empire, and Aramaic remained the common language of the Jews up to the time of Jesus.

To complicate matters, Alexander the Great conquered the Persian Empire and when he died in 323 BC, Palestine and Egypt came under the control of Alexander's former general Ptolemy I, and then his son, Ptolemy II. During their reigns, the official language of Palestine and Egypt was Greek. Because so few Jews understood much Hebrew, translations of the Hebrew Scriptures were made – first into Aramaic and then into Greek. At a later time, a Syriac translation was made.

This woodcut depicts the hall in the library of Alexandria.

Targums: Scripture in Jesus' Language

Upon returning to Jerusalem from exile around 458 BC, the priest and scribe Ezra had called the people together to read the book of the law. Realizing that few in his audience understood Hebrew, he first read the Hebrew text, then had someone repeat what he had just read in Aramaic.

This practice became customary. During synagogue services one man read from the Scriptures in Hebrew and another gave a translation or interpretation of the reading in Aramaic. These Aramaic versions came to be called *targums* (Hebrew for "translation" or "interpretation").

Jesus himself would participate in such a service in Nazareth. According to Luke 4:16–20, a synagogue official handed Jesus a scroll of Isaiah and asked him to read. Jesus read from the scroll, then preached on it. It is likely that Jesus, whose native language was Aramaic, followed local custom by reading from a targum.

In the beginning the targums were preserved by word of mouth. Later they were written down and frequently revised. By the early Christian era, there were targums for the entire Jewish Bible except for the books of Ezra, Nehemiah, and Daniel.

Some of these targums were close translations, while others paraphrased Scripture or incorporated additional material. Today scholars often use the Aramaic word in a targum to ascertain the correct word in a damaged or blurred Hebrew manuscript of the same passage. Targums also give us an idea of early Jewish interpretations of the texts.

The Septuagint

Ptolemy II was a great ruler who fostered learning. His capital at Alexandria, Egypt, with its great library, became a major centre of learning that attracted many Jews, among others. These Jews worked and studied in the Greek language, received a Greek education, and adopted many Greek customs. In response to their need for a Greek version of their Scriptures, a translation of the Pentateuch appeared about 250 BC.

According to an ancient manuscript, the *Letter of Aristeas*, Ptolemy himself was responsible for the translation. Wanting a Greek version of the Hebrew law for his library, he sent to Jerusalem for 72 Jewish scholars (6 from each of the 12 tribes

As the books were read, the priests stood up… and said, "Since this version has been made rightly and reverently, and in every respect accurately, it is good that this should remain exactly so, and there should be no revision."

LETTER OF ARISTEAS

of Israel). In Alexandria the scholars divided the work among themselves, consulting one another as they progressed, and translated the Pentateuch in 72 days.

The translation came to be called the Septuagint ("seventy") for the roughly seventy translators. In a variation on the story of its origins, the first-century Jewish philosopher Philo held that each of the 72 scholars, working independently, translated the entire text of the Pentateuch, producing 72 identical texts.

Although the stories of its origins are probably not authentic, a Greek translation of the Pentateuch was indeed made, followed over the next century or two by the remaining books of the Hebrew Scriptures. The Septuagint became the standard Greek translation of the Jewish Bible and was the version the New Testament writers used.

The Septuagint may have been commissioned by Ptolemy II, shown left with his sister (and later wife), Arsinoe II.

Manuscript pages from a thirteenth-century copy of the Peshitta, the official Bible of the Syrian Orthodox and Maronite Churches.

Variations from the Official Hebrew Bible

Because the official Jewish version of the Hebrew Bible was established sometime after the completion of the Septuagint, there are differences. Most importantly, the Septuagint contains books that are not found in the standard Bible. These include the books of the Apocrypha (found in some Christian Bibles), the Psalms of Solomon – a collection of psalms from the first century BC, which sing of a messiah who will conquer Israel's enemies – and odes – a collection of 15 songs or prayers, most of which are repeated from elsewhere in the Bible. Finally, 3 Maccabees comforts Jews of Alexandria during a persecution, and 4 Maccabees gives a history of the Jews from 184 to 86 BC.

There are also major variations in the contents of the books. For example, Job is shorter in the Septuagint than in the standard text, while Jeremiah is 20 per cent longer, suggesting that the book went through two or more versions.

Today, earlier Greek versions of a text can help scholars understand unclear Hebrew passages, and so the Septuagint remains important in helping Christians fully understand the word of God.

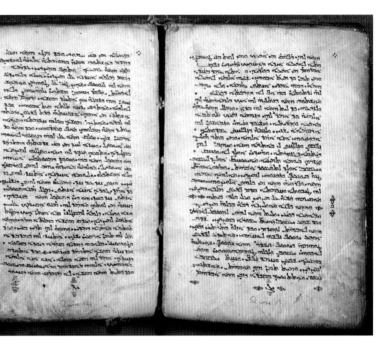

The Peshitta: The Bible in a New Tongue

Shortly before the birth of Jesus, Syriac, a new language closely related to Aramaic, developed in and around Edessa (modern Urfa in south-eastern Turkey). In the first and second centuries AD, the Jewish Bible was translated into Syriac and later called *peshitta* ("pure") to distinguish it from later Syriac translations made from the Greek Septuagint. The books of the Peshitta were created by different writers in different places, but all were completed by the end of the first century or shortly after. New Testament translations were added to the Peshitta in the second century.

Some of the books of the Peshitta show the influence of the Aramaic targums. Because Syriac and Aramaic relate closely to the Hebrew language, scholars sometimes use copies of the Peshitta and some targums to establish correct texts for obscure Hebrew readings.

Settling the Jewish Bible

ESTABLISHING WHAT'S IN AND WHAT'S OUT

While Christians use the term "Old Testament" for the Jewish Scriptures, Jews generally use *Tanakh*, or *TNK*, an acronym for the three parts of the Jewish Bible: *Torah* (Law), *Nevi'im* (Prophets), and *Ketuvim* (Writings).

There are 24 books in the Jewish canon. "Canon" is a Greek word meaning "measuring rod", because the books in a canon "measure up" to a standard of excellence – in this case, including divine inspiration.

Although nothing certain is known about how or when the books of the Old Testament were chosen, the canon seems to have been approved one section at a time, in the order described by Jesus: "the law of Moses, the prophets and the psalms", with psalms referring to the Writings, of which Psalms is the first and longest book (Luke 24:44). It probably took the Jews centuries to settle on which books to include in their Bible – from about 600 BC to the first century AD.

Accepting the Law
• •
It is generally believed that the books of the Torah were authoritatively accepted as the laws and teachings of God and given their final form during or just after the Babylonian exile. It may be that Ezra's reading of the law to the people of Jerusalem after the exile was meant to officially establish the books as Jewish law. From that point on, it is believed, the Torah was considered the heart of Jewish Scripture.

Accepting the Prophets
• •
Scholars say the long process of canonizing the books of the Prophets probably began in the fifth century BC – about the time Malachi, the last book in this section, was written.

In the Jewish Bible, the prophetic books are divided into two categories: Former and Latter Prophets. The Former Prophets may have been accepted first, since they are books about early Jewish history. The Latter Prophets were books from later times and deal more with the ministries of individual prophets, including their teachings. They include three long books – Isaiah, Jeremiah, and Ezekiel – and a collection of shorter prophetic books, grouped together and named the Twelve.

Jews carrying a Torah scroll to be read at a bar mitzvah ceremony in Jerusalem. The Torah, a collection of the first five books of the Bible, is considered especially important because it contains God's laws.

Accepting the Writings and Closing the Canon
• •
The remaining books, collectively known as the Writings, were surely the last to be canonized. The earliest mention of a Jewish Bible containing 24 books appears in 2 Esdras, a Jewish work written in the first century AD and included in the Apocrypha. Josephus, a first-century Jewish historian, says there were 22 books, but he was probably combining Ruth and Judges (whose stories take place in the same era) and Jeremiah and Lamentations (both thought to have been written by Jeremiah).

SEE ALSO
THE SEPTUAGINT, PP. 24–25
THE APOCRYPHA, PP. 28–29

> *Make public the twenty-four books that you wrote first, and let the worthy and the unworthy read them.*
>
> **2 ESDRAS 14:45**

Other Jewish writings appeared on the scene too late to be included in the Writings. A number of them, however, were included in the Septuagint. In Protestant Bibles, these books are omitted or are grouped together as the Apocrypha, the Greek word for "hidden".

Some scholars say the canon of the Jewish Bible was closed late in the first century AD by Jewish leaders convened at the Council of Jamnia. Other scholars insist no such council meeting ever took place.

The order of books in the Jewish Bible does not match the order of Old Testament books in Christian Bibles. In Christian Bibles, for example, Daniel is among the prophets, and Chronicles comes after Kings as a history book. Most importantly, the books considered the later prophets by the Jews are placed last in Christian Bibles, as their words look forward to the New Testament where they will be fulfilled.

The Samaritan Bible: Rival Scriptures

Samaritans are the descendants of the Assyrian invaders who took over northern Israel in the eighth century BC and married the surviving Jews. In late Bible times Jews considered them to be a pagan people of mixed race and distorted faith – though the Samaritans counter that they were the only faithful remnant of Israel and guardians of the true scripture.

The Samaritans considered only the first five books of the Bible sacred, but their version of those books identifies Mount Gerizim – not Jerusalem – as the proper place to worship God. Several hundred Samaritans still live in Israel, and they claim to have a copy of the Pentateuch signed by Abisha, the great grandson of Aaron – Moses' brother and Israel's first high priest. Critics question the authenticity of the signature and consider the Abisha scroll a patchwork of fragments written over many centuries.

BOOKS OF THE CANON

The Jewish Bible and the Protestant Old Testament are the same, although they are arranged in a different order. Roman Catholic and Eastern Orthodox Bibles include several additional books, known as the Apocrypha. Those books appeared in the Septuagint, an early Greek translation of Jewish Scripture, but they were later dropped by the Jews – and Protestants later followed suit.

The Abisha scroll, the most sacred relic among Samaritans. This scroll of the Samaritan Bible is signed by Abisha, who claims to be the great-grandson of Aaron, the brother of Moses. But scholars date the lettering style to about 2,500 years after Aaron.

The Jewish Scriptures (24 Books)

The Law	The Writings
Genesis	Psalms
Exodus	Job
Leviticus	Proverbs
Numbers	Ruth
Deuteronomy	Song of Solomon
The Prophets	Ecclesiastes
Former Prophets	Lamentations
Joshua	Esther
Judges	Daniel
Samuel	Ezra-Nehemiah
Kings	Chronicles
Latter Prophets	
Isaiah	
Jeremiah	
Ezekiel	
The Twelve (the collection of Hosea, Joel, Amos, Obadiah, Jonah, Micah, Nahum, Habakkuk, Zephaniah, Haggai, Zechariah and Malachi)	

Protestant Old Testament (39 Books)

History	Prophecy
Genesis	Isaiah
Exodus	Jeremiah
Leviticus	Lamentations
Numbers	Ezekiel
Deuteronomy	Daniel
Joshua	Hosea
Judges	Joel
Ruth	Amos
1, 2 Samuel	Obadiah
1, 2 Kings	Jonah
1, 2 Chronicles	Micah
Ezra	Nahum
Nehemiah	Habakkuk
Esther	Zephaniah
Poetry	Haggai
Job	Zechariah
Psalms	Malachi
Proverbs	
Ecclesiastes	
Song of Solomon	

Falling Between the Testaments

THE APOCRYPHA AND OTHER WORKS

The books of the Hebrew Bible were not the only revered Jewish texts. There were dozens of other respected works, which fall into two groups. The first group contains works that were included in the Septuagint, the Greek translation of the Bible, but not in the later canon. Most of these writings are included in the Old Testament by Catholic and Eastern churches, but are not considered canonical by Protestants, who call them the Apocrypha. The second group of non-canonical writings consists of more than 50 works of a diverse nature. They are supplemented by Jewish histories that reach into the early Christian era and refer to John the Baptist and Jesus.

The Apocrypha

The books of the Apocrypha, written between 300 BC and AD 70, include the romantic stories of Tobit and Judith, histories, and books of wisdom.

■ Tobit tells of an old man of Nineveh who defies the Assyrian king by burying an executed fellow Jew. Tobit loses his wealth and is blinded by bird droppings. His son, Tobias, travels to Media, and collects money owed to Tobit. Along the way Tobias meets Sarah, who has married seven times only to have each husband murdered by a demon on their wedding night. Tobias kills the demon, marries Sarah, returns home, and restores his father's eyesight using the gall of a man-eating fish. Tobit, who risked everything to give a neighbour a decent burial, is a model of the charitable man.

■ Judith tells of a Jewish heroine who helps her people defeat the Assyrians by single-handedly beheading the Assyrian leader, Holofernes.

Susanna and the Two Elders by Lorenzo Lotto (c. 1480–1556). In the story of Susanna, two Jewish elders try to pressure Susanna into sex. When she refuses, they accuse her of sleeping with a young man. Daniel defends her and exposes the lie.

■ 1 and 2 Maccabees relate the history of the Hasmonean family who overthrew the Seleucids (Syrians) in the second century BC and ruled the Jews until the Romans came in 63 BC. They were called the Maccabees (Greek for "hammer") because their leader Judas struck his enemies like a hammer.

■ Sirach presents the teaching of the scholar Jesus Ben Sira, who uses proverbs and poems to teach wisdom, which he equates with the fulfilment of God's law.

■ Wisdom of Solomon personifies Wisdom as the saviour of Israel's ancestors and promises immortality to the righteous, a concept that would be important to Christians.

And then the two men lifted me up to the seventh heaven. There I saw a great light and fiery troops of great archangels, bodiless forces, dominions, orders, governments, cherubim and seraphim, thrones and multi-eyed beings, nine regiments of them... and the Lord at a distance, sitting on his high throne.

2 Enoch 20:1–2

■ Baruch tells how the prophet Jeremiah's scribe wrote texts to be read at the Jerusalem temple, encouraging the exiles in Babylon and reproaching Israel for forsaking God's law. A letter to those exiles, which is attributed to Jeremiah, is sometimes included, sometimes presented separately.

■ Additions to the book of Esther include plot developments, a dream, and prayers. Though the canonical book never mentions God, the additions do frequently.

■ Additions to Daniel include songs, prayers, and stories, including the one of Susannah and the Elders.

Pseudo Writings

Other books that did not make it into the Bible are pseudepigrapha, or "pseudo" writings. Dating to between 200 BC and AD 200, many imitated earlier biblical books or were written under an authoritative pseudonym – such as Moses, Solomon, or Isaiah.

About 20 of these belong to the type of visionary work known as apocalyptic. Most notable are the three books of Enoch, which speak of eternal life for the righteous and tell the story of the fallen angels alluded to in Genesis 6:1–4.

The pseudepigrapha also include extensions of biblical stories, including the story of Jannes and Jambres, the Egyptian magicians who opposed Moses. There are also testaments of Old Testament figures, such as "The Testament of the Twelve Patriarchs", in which each of Jacob's sons gives moral advice as he nears death. Finally, there are books of wisdom, prayers and hymns, and various fragments.

Josephus, Jewish Historian

Apart from the above, a first-century Jew wrote several volumes of history that fill in the gaps between the Old and New Testaments. Flavius Josephus, who was born in Jerusalem, led rebel forces against the occupying Romans in AD 67. He was captured by the Roman commander Vespasian, gained favour by predicting that Vespasian would become emperor, then served as aide to Vespasian's son, Titus, when the Romans crushed the Jewish rebellion in AD 70, looting and destroying the temple.

Considered a traitor at home, Josephus

This panel from the Arch of Titus in Rome depicts Roman soldiers in triumphant procession, carrying the menorah and other artefacts looted from the Jerusalem temple before its destruction in AD 70. Josephus witnessed the event and wrote about it.

spent his final years in Rome, writing. His most significant works are *The Jewish War*, a history of the revolt he had experienced, and *The Antiquities of the Jews*, a review of Jewish history from the creation to his own time. These histories give new perspectives on biblical events and throw light on Josephus's own time.

Along the way, Josephus describes the Essenes, Jews who broke away from the Jerusalem establishment to live in the desert, copy the Scriptures, and write their own intriguing works – works that were to remain unknown until the Dead Sea Scrolls were discovered in the twentieth century.

Josephus also touches on three New Testament figures. He confirms the Bible's claim that Herod Agrippa executed John the Baptist; he describes the martyrdom of James the brother of Jesus; and, most dramatically, he identifies Jesus as the resurrected Messiah. Unfortunately, these passages were preserved by Christians, who seem to have bolstered the claims made by Josephus of Jesus' divinity. The unedited text has not survived.

Josephus, depicted in a copper engraving from 1737.

Spreading the Good News

THE BEGINNINGS OF CHRISTIANITY

Jesus of Nazareth was born about 6 BC. Some 30 years later he engaged in a ministry of teaching and healing, then was arrested and put to death as a criminal. But three days later Jesus rose from the dead, and his disciples realized that he was the Messiah promised by the prophets. At first, no one wrote anything down about Jesus, but Jesus' followers spread the word about him among themselves. For example, on the Sunday after the crucifixion, as two of Jesus' followers were walking to the village of Emmaus, near Jerusalem, and "talking about all that had happened" (Luke 24:14), they met the risen Jesus, whom they did not recognize.

When Jesus asked what they were discussing, they sadly told the story of how Jesus had been condemned and crucified, dashing their hopes that he was the Messiah. Though some women had found Jesus' tomb empty that morning and were told by angels that Jesus had risen from the dead, this seemed unlikely. Jesus admonished the disciples for not believing. When they recognized him, their doubts vanished and they rushed back to Jerusalem to tell their story to the others.

A Christian Oral Tradition

The incident on the road to Emmaus illustrates how stories about Jesus must have been passed along in the early years of Christianity. Men and women who had known Jesus would describe or proclaim what they had witnessed to everyone they met, spreading the good news of Jesus by word of mouth. The first proclamations about Jesus were simple and direct. Jesus had died and was raised from the dead. More elaborate ones, such as the first sermon of Jesus' chief disciple, Peter (Acts 2:14–36), identified Jesus as the Messiah and showed how the prophets had foretold his death and resurrection. Later proclamations pointed out that Jesus had died for the forgiveness of our sins and would come again in glory to judge the living and the dead. These basic proclamations were eventually formed into short creeds that were used to teach and to recite at baptisms.

But, eager for details, people probably gathered around Jesus' disciples to hear stories about him as the earlier Hebrews had gathered around storytellers to hear about the creation and the flood. Soon after, fuller accounts of Jesus' resurrection and of his trial and death probably surfaced. To these were added memories of his miraculous healings, and, of course, the sayings of Jesus were repeated.

No Need to Write

Early Christians saw no need to write about Jesus, who had himself left behind no writings. For one thing, Jesus' early followers did not consider themselves part of a new religion that needed its own scriptures. They were mostly good Jews who accepted the Hebrew Scriptures and believed that Jesus had fulfilled those Scriptures. Gentiles who followed Jesus adopted Judaism as their religion.

At any rate, these early Christians also believed that Jesus would soon come again, so they saw no reason to write anything down. They could keep the traditions about Jesus alive by word of mouth until he returned again to bring his kingdom to completion.

Jesus flanked by Peter and Paul, with Andrew and John, in a Byzantine mosaic of the sixth century.

● SEE ALSO
THE ORAL TRADITION, PP. 8–9
WRITING DOWN THE GOOD NEWS,
PP. 34–35

Let the entire house of Israel know with certainty that God has made him both Lord and Messiah, this Jesus whom you crucified.

PROCLAMATION OF THE APOSTLE PETER, ACTS 2:36

Grouping the Jesus Traditions

The earliest accounts of Jesus were related by those who had known him personally. In time, others began to spread the good news.

In order to organize the traditions about Jesus, the second generation of teachers often grouped them together. For example, they kept accounts of Jesus' actions separate from his sayings. There were stories about Jesus' baptism or his passion and death, and stories about his miracles. The miracle stories were in turn broken down into nature miracles (such as calming the storm) and healings.

Jesus' sayings were similarly grouped by type. One type of sayings, the parables, were often told in clusters of three, sometimes sharing a theme, such as sowing seed.

It is possible that some early collections of stories of Jesus' actions and sayings were written down and may have been used later by the authors of the Gospels.

Fitting the Format

As stories about Jesus were told and retold, they were often restructured to fit specific patterns. For example, stories of healings followed a format used in the Old Testament: (1) the ailment is described; (2) the afflicted person asks for a cure; (3) the healing is accomplished through words or touch; (4) proof of the healing is supplied; (5) the spectators are amazed. The healing of the leper in Mark 1:40–45 follows this structure.

Often the incidents from Jesus' life were made to follow these formats even if the facts had to be carefully chosen, rearranged, or even elaborated to make them fit the mould. This was not a distortion of the truth, for the storyteller's intention was not to give a detailed description of Jesus' actions, but rather to point out the power Jesus had over life and death, health and disease. By fitting a story about Jesus into a recognizable form, the central message of the story was made clear to those who heard the good news.

While spreading the good news by word of mouth, Philip, one of Jesus' apostles, converts and baptizes an Ethiopian eunuch.

Keeping in Touch

PAUL'S LETTERS TO THE CHURCHES

St. Paul Preaching Before the Temple of Diana at Ephesus, a painting by Adolph Pirsch (1858–1929).

In about AD 50, some 20 years after Jesus' resurrection, Paul of Tarsus, who had been travelling widely to spread the good news of Jesus to everyone, began to write letters to churches he had helped to establish. The letters that survive constitute a large part of the New Testament. Some of them are the earliest Christian writings to survive.

Paul had not always been a Christian. Earlier, as a strict Jew, he had actually persecuted followers of Jesus, regarding them as blasphemers who thwarted Mosaic law and rashly accepted a crucified carpenter as the Messiah. Then, in AD 35, Paul had a blinding personal vision of Jesus. From then on, though he suffered imprisonment and other abuses, he devoted all his energies to bringing Jesus into the lives of others, especially Gentiles (non-Jews). He was stopped only by an executioner's sword.

From Sermons to Letters

Following his vision Paul took time out to adjust and to learn from the apostles, who initially resisted him. He was encouraged by Barnabas, another Jewish Christian, and spent a year with him ministering to a mixed congregation of Jews and Gentiles in Antioch, Syria. In AD 46 Paul and Barnabas became missionaries.

Paul made three missionary journeys, during which he covered some 10,000 miles throughout the Middle East and southern Europe. Wherever he stopped, Paul preached about Jesus at the synagogues and in public arenas, attracting a few Jews, but even more Gentiles, to follow the way of Jesus. Generally, he stayed in a town a few days or weeks, forming a community, or church, and teaching the basics of Christianity.

On his second journey, Paul realized that after he left a town, disagreements sometimes erupted, or newcomers offered different slants on the gospel message, confusing and dividing the new churches. Sometimes the churches sent messengers with questions. Paul responded by writing letters. About half the books of the New Testament are letters – most of them from Paul.

The Letters Themselves

Paul's letters are probably the oldest books in the New Testament, written before the first two Gospels. Many scholars say that 1 Thessalonians is the oldest. After Paul left Thessalonica, during his second missionary journey in about AD 50, the believers apparently sent him a message. They were confused about Jesus' second coming, and they were worried about what would happen to believers who died before Jesus came back. Paul assured the believers that when Jesus returns, "the dead in Christ will rise first" (1 Thessalonians 4:16).

Other letters responded to other questions and other problems in other communities. The letter to the Romans differed in that Paul had not founded the church there nor even visited. Paul was writing to introduce himself and to present his views. Consequently, Romans is the most theological of all of Paul's letters. In contrast, Philemon is purely personal – though it speaks to all of us. It is basically a note asking the Christian Philemon to free his slave Onesimus as an act of love.

Which Letters Did Paul Write?

Thirteen letters claim Paul as their writer. A fourteenth – Hebrews – has sometimes been attributed to him as well, although he almost certainly did not write it.

Exactly which letters Paul wrote is a matter of debate. It was common in ancient times for students to write under the name of their mentor, as a means of honouring them by applying their teachings to new situations. That is what may have happened with books such as 1 and 2 Timothy and Titus, which are different from Paul's other letters in tone and writing style. Because these letters deal largely with matters of church administration, they are generally called the Pastoral Letters.

By about a century after Paul's death, his letters were being collected and bound into individual books, and then circulated throughout the church. The earliest known copies usually included 10 or 11 letters, sometimes including Hebrews and sometimes excluding 1 and 2 Timothy along with Titus. Paul's letters were generally arranged in order of length, from longest to shortest: Romans, Hebrews, 1 and 2 Corinthians, Ephesians, Galatians, Philippians, Colossians, 1 and 2 Thessalonians, and Philemon.

In time, the order of Galatians and Ephesians was switched, the letters to Timothy and Titus were added and put in front of the shorter letter to Philemon, and Hebrews was moved to the end, because it did not identify the writer.

HOW TO WRITE A LETTER

Like today's business letters, formal Greek letters in Paul's time followed a distinct format. Although he felt free to adapt it, Paul generally used the following format:

- **Opening**: Identification of the writer and the recipient, followed by the word "Greetings". Paul generally opened with a blessing, such as "Grace to you and peace from God our Father and the Lord Jesus Christ" (Romans 1:7).

- **Introduction**: Thanks are given to the gods. Paul gave thanks to God, but sometimes he also offered short prayers for the recipients or praised them. "I give thanks to my God always for you" (1 Corinthians 1:4). In his stern letter to the Galatians Paul skipped the customary, polite introduction and jumped right to his main point, declaring he was shocked that the people had already rejected the true gospel he had taught them.

- **Body**: The main message, often introduced with a concise statement about the letter's purpose. Paul followed this pattern in 1 Corinthians, where he appealed to the church members to stop arguing (1 Corinthians 1:10).

- **Closing**: Wishes for the recipient's good health and a "Farewell". Paul, instead, closed his letters with a benediction, a short prayer of blessing and hope, such as: "The grace of the Lord Jesus Christ, the love of God, and the communion of the Holy Spirit be with all of you" (2 Corinthians 13:14).

Paul wrote letters to churches in the cities shown on this map, as well as to churches scattered throughout the territory of Galatia, in what is now Turkey.

33

Writing Down the Good News

THE GOSPELS OF MARK AND MATTHEW

In the mid 60s, most of the traditions about Jesus were still being passed on by word of mouth, and many of the men and women who had known Jesus had died. At the same time, it was becoming obvious that Jesus' second coming was not imminent. In his letters, Paul touched on events in Jesus' life, and some of Jesus' words and deeds may have been copied into a few collections by the early 60s, but nothing more. A structured account of Jesus' words and deeds was needed. Between AD 68 and 73, the Gospel According to Mark appeared, filling that need.

Mark Makes His Mark

Although the Gospel According to Matthew appears first in the New Testament, Mark's Gospel was probably written first, as it seems to have served as a major source for the Gospels of Matthew and Luke. According to an early tradition, the author of this Gospel was John Mark, an aide to Paul and an associate of the apostle Peter, who may have supplied material for the Gospel. Mark's other sources were disconnected memories, tales, sayings, and a few lengthier narratives. Mark gathered these materials into a cohesive whole with a point of view that was almost surely influenced by the situation of the Christians for whom he was writing. Mark indicates that the situation was perilous by including Jesus' prediction that his followers would face persecution. This suggests that Mark wrote his Gospel in Rome soon after Peter was martyred there in AD 64. If so, Mark may have been preparing his Roman readers for facing persecution and even death, emphasizing the need to take up one's cross. The cross, in fact, is at the centre of Mark's Gospel.

Mark structured his work by grouping together events that occurred in Galilee, on the way to Jerusalem, and, finally, in Jerusalem. Much of Mark's Gospel is taken up by his account of Jesus' passion and death. The original Gospel ended abruptly with the women at Jesus' empty tomb saying nothing, "for they were afraid" (Mark 16:8). It is believed that scribes, bothered by this ending, later added the verses about Jesus' post-resurrection appearances that are now found in Mark 16:9–20, drawn from the other Gospels.

Sixth-century mosaic of Mark the evangelist.

Matthew Follows Mark and Fills out the Story

Copies of Mark's Gospel were widespread and served as a source for later Gospels. The first of these, the Gospel of Matthew, incorporates most of Mark's text, sometimes rewriting it, often repeating it word for word, but also making additions about Jesus' birth and infancy and about his appearances after the resurrection. There are also five added discourses, or sermons, including the Sermon on the Mount, which features the Beatitudes and the Lord's Prayer, and a description of the Last Judgment in which Jesus separates the sheep from the goats (the saved from the damned) by judging whether or not individuals took care of the needy.

Because much of the material in the discourses also appears in the Gospel of Luke, but not in Mark, scholars have speculated that Matthew drew this material from a lost collection of Jesus' sayings, which they have named Q from the word *Quelle* (German for "source"). Whether or not there was a Q, Matthew – and later Luke – apparently used material from several written and oral sources, including material that is found neither in Mark nor in the supposed Q.

MATTHEW'S JEWISH POINT OF VIEW

Each of the Gospel writers wrote for members of their own church, responding to the community's needs. Most of Mark's first readers were probably Gentile Christians, as Mark usually explains Aramaic terms and Jewish customs, but not Latin words or Roman customs. On the other hand, Matthew's community must have been heavily Jewish, for the Gospel emphasizes respect for the Jewish law and doesn't explain Jewish customs. Matthew also makes heavy use of the Old Testament and repeatedly shows how Jesus fulfils Old Testament prophecies.

Mark became Peter's interpreter and wrote accurately all that he remembered of the things said and done by the Lord, but not in order, for he had not heard the Lord.

PAPIAS IN EUSEBIUS'S *HISTORY OF THE CHURCH*

● SEE ALSO
SPREADING THE GOOD NEWS, PP. 30–31
MORE GOSPELS – AND ACTS, PP. 36–37

According to an early tradition, Matthew, the tax collector whom Jesus called as an apostle, wrote this Gospel – probably about AD 85 in Antioch. Whereas Mark's Gospel emphasizes the acceptance of suffering, Matthew's emphasizes the church. Rooted in the teaching of Jesus, the church is built on rock and "the gates of Hades will not prevail against it" (Matthew 16:18). Matthew's Gospel quickly became the primary teaching tool of the church, which may account for it being positioned as the first book of the New Testament.

Chapter 25 of Matthew's Gospel describes the Last Judgment, shown here in a fresco by Giotto di Bondone.

GREEK WORDS IN THE BIBLE

As in English, Greek has capital letters and lower case letters. Early Bible manuscripts used mainly capital letters, like those shown here:

Greek Word	Pronunciation (transliteration)	English Translation
ΘΕΟΣ	Theos	God
᾽ΙΗΣΟΥΣ	Iesous	Jesus
ΧΡΙΣΤΟΣ	Christos	Messiah
ΑΓΑΠΗ	agapé	love

Three Stages of Development

By the time the Gospels were finally written they had gone through three stages of development: (1) there were eyewitness accounts from those who knew Jesus; (2) these accounts were shaped and focused by the needs of the early Christian communities; (3) an individual in one of those communities reshaped the material in writing to best suit the needs of his first readers. In addition, the authors of the Gospels must have had to translate some of their source material from Aramaic into Greek, the language of the New Testament.

Languages of Jesus' Day

Four languages were used in New Testament times: Hebrew, Aramaic, Greek, and Latin. Jesus and most others in Israel spoke Aramaic, which the Jews had adopted from their captors during the Babylonian exile. Hebrew was reserved mainly for priests and rabbis. The occupying Romans used Latin for proclamations and inscriptions, but when abroad they used Greek.

Greek became the dominant language of the Near East after Alexander the Great conquered most of the Mediterranean world in the fourth century BC and it remained so in Jesus' time. Because Greek was so widely understood, the Jewish Scriptures had been translated into Greek (the Septuagint) and the New Testament writers followed suit.

More Gospels – and Acts

LUKE STRESSES INCLUSIVENESS; JOHN STRESSES LOVE

The Gospels attributed to Luke and John are different from one another, yet similar. While Luke follows the format initiated by Mark, he emphasizes Jesus' love for everyone – Jew, Gentile, man, woman, saint, sinner, everyone. Luke also adds a second part to his Gospel, which is a history of the early church – the Acts of the Apostles. John, on the other hand, abandons Mark's format and writes a more theological work, examining who Jesus is. He concludes that in sending Jesus to earth to die for us, God shows that he is love itself. So, in a way, both Luke and John emphasize the love God has for us all.

MATTHEW, MARK, AND LUKE

Because the first three Gospels are so similar, they are called the Synoptic Gospels to distinguish them from the Gospel of John. The term "synoptic", from the Greek for "seen together", refers to the fact that scholars examine them side by side to study the relationship of one to the other.

Luke's Double Gospel

The third Gospel is actually in two volumes – the Gospel proper and the Acts of the Apostles, a volume that continues the story of the early church after Jesus' ascension. The two books are written in a masterful Greek style that is carefully organized, drawing many parallels between the ministry of Jesus and that of Paul.

Like Matthew, Luke used much of Mark's Gospel, adding material of his own. Like Matthew, Luke has an infancy narrative, but he tells it from Mary's perspective while Matthew had told his from Joseph's perception and related it to the Old Testament. Luke also adds material on Jesus' ministry in Galilee, which includes the Sermon on the Plain, a shorter version of Matthew's Sermon on the Mount. Another added second section (Luke 9:51–18:14) describes Jesus' journey from Galilee to Jerusalem to face death. Included in this section are the otherwise unknown parables of the Good Samaritan and the Prodigal Son. The Gospel ends with stories of Jesus' appearances after his resurrection.

Acts tells the story of the early church from the ascension to Paul's arrival in Rome. Thus it moves from Jerusalem, the centre of the Jewish world, to Rome, the centre of the Gentile world, underlining Luke's main theme, that Jesus came for all – men and women, saints and sinners, Jews and Gentiles alike.

The oldest surviving manuscripts of the third Gospel attribute it to Luke, who may be the companion that Paul refers to as "the beloved physician" (Colossians 4:14). Luke was probably a Gentile convert from Antioch. He wrote his Gospel around AD 85 for a community made up of mainly Gentile Christians, as the text avoids Jewish expressions and customs that would be unfamiliar to non-Jews, and the thrust of Luke's text is to spread the good news to Gentiles as well as Jews, extending Jesus' message to all people far and wide.

Fourteenth-century icons depicting Luke (left) and John (below), the evangelists.

● SEE ALSO
WRITING DOWN THE GOOD NEWS,
PP. 34–35

> *I too decided, after investigating everything carefully from the very first, to write an orderly account for you, most excellent Theophilus, so that you may know the truth concerning the things about which you have been instructed.*
> LUKE 1:3–4

IS JOHN'S GOSPEL ANTI-SEMITIC?

Because John's Gospel often speaks of "the Jews" with seeming animosity, many readers have regarded the Gospel as anti-Semitic. This is not so. Most of the Christians in the community that produced the Gospel were themselves Jews who had come to believe in Jesus. Because they believed in the divinity of Jesus, however, they scandalized other Jews who saw them as violating the first commandment – the worship of only one God. In time the traditionalist Jews expelled the Christians from their synagogues. Although they still followed Jewish law, the Christians began to regard the Jews who expelled them as the other side, equating them with the ones who rejected Jesus. The Gospel, then, uses the term "the Jews" to describe only Jews who specifically rejected Jesus (not all Jews).

The Fourth Gospel

The fourth Gospel, and the last to be written, is a more poetic and theological work than the others. The Gospel itself tells us that the author was the (unnamed) "disciple whom Jesus loved" (John 21:20). Since the second century, he has generally been identified as the apostle John, though many scholars feel that the Gospel was actually written by one or more of the followers of the beloved disciple, rather than the apostle himself.

The first 11 chapters of John's Gospel are structured around seven miracles, most of which are not recorded elsewhere. John calls these miracles "signs", because they point to some aspect of Jesus' identity. Typically, Jesus performs a miracle, or sign, that involves a dialogue in which Jesus makes a proclamation about himself – for example, before raising Lazarus from the dead he proclaims: "I am the resurrection and the life" (John 11:25). The remainder of the Gospel relates Jesus' arrest, death, and resurrection.

What is Truth?

Sceptics have pointed out inconsistencies in the Gospels that seem to undermine their accuracy. But the Gospel writers were not trying to set down a chronology of Jesus' life. They were writing theological works that showed who and what Jesus was. They saw nothing wrong with changing a historical fact to make a theological point. For example, in the Gospels of Matthew, Mark, and Luke, Jesus' last supper with his disciples is a Passover meal, commemorating the last meal the Israelites ate before fleeing Egypt. In John's Gospel, this last supper is eaten the day before Passover. Why the difference? The first three Gospels present the Last Supper as a Passover meal in which the traditional bread and wine become the body and blood of Jesus. John, on the other hand, sees Jesus as the lamb that is to be eaten at the Passover feast, and so he has Jesus die at the time the paschal lamb would be slaughtered, thereby changing the day. The evangelists, then, were giving symbolic meaning to the meal. They had little regard for the day it was eaten. Each Gospel shows aspects of Jesus and what he means to us. The truth of historical detail is less important than the overall "truth" the Gospels seek to teach.

This fragment from the Gospel of John from about AD 125 is the oldest surviving copy of any part of the New Testament.

Other Christian Letters

LETTERS NOT WRITTEN BY PAUL

Paul wrote to individuals and congregations. A number of other early Christian leaders wrote what scholars call "General Letters" because they were intended for circulation among a general audience of Christians. They are James, 1 and 2 Peter, 1, 2, and 3 John, Jude, and – possibly – Hebrews.

Although the General Letters and Pauline Letters (those probably written by Paul) were written by different people, at different times and for different reasons, they all share a common purpose: to inspire and help fellow Christians come closer to God.

Letter of James

Because it is full of advice about how to live a godly life, the Letter of James is considered to be the Proverbs of the New Testament. Exactly who is giving this advice remains unclear. The writer identifies himself only as "James, a servant of God and of the Lord Jesus Christ" (James 1:1). There are four men named James in the New Testament, but at least since the fourth century AD, church leaders have attributed the letter to the James the Gospels identify as a brother of Jesus (Matthew 13:55; Mark 6:3), and that Acts and Paul's letters identify as leader of the Jerusalem church. If this James was the writer, the letter was written before AD 62, for James was stoned to death in that year.

1 and 2 Peter

1 Peter was written to encourage Christians facing persecution, perhaps in the early 60s, when Christians became increasingly viewed as a radical cult instead of a legitimate branch of the Jewish religion. It could also have been written later, after Nero accused Christians of setting fire to Rome in AD 64.

The writer identifies himself as the apostle Peter, but some scholars doubt Peter wrote the letter because the writing style is refined Greek, a surprising feat for a Galilean fisherman. Other scholars say Peter admitted he had help: "Through Silvanus, whom I consider a faithful brother, I have written this short letter" (1 Peter 5:12). Silvanus (Silas in Greek) was a Christian who travelled with Paul (Acts 15:22). Scholars who doubt that Peter wrote this letter say the persecution could have been during the 90s, long after Peter's death.

However, writing in about AD 95 Clement, a church leader in Rome who was later known as Pope Clement I, referred to 1 Peter, as did Irenaeus, a second-century church leader, who added that Peter wrote it.

Written to warn Christians about heretical teachers, 2 Peter has the feel of a last testament from someone about to die. The writer, who identifies himself as the apostle Peter, says he has received word from heaven that he will die soon.

As early as the second century, church leaders began to doubt Peter's authorship of 2 Peter, for the writing style is dramatically different from 1 Peter, with less refined Greek. There are striking similarities with Jude, however, both in content and wording. Finally, the writer implies that Paul's letters are already revered, because he associates them with "other scriptures" (2 Peter 3:16). This leads some scholars to suggest that 2 Peter was written in Peter's name by a follower and was perhaps the last New Testament book written – possibly as late as AD 100 to 150.

1, 2, and 3 John

The three short letters of John seem to reflect a time when Jewish believers in Christ had been banned from worshipping with other Jews – an action taken by many synagogues in the late first century. The first two letters help Christians deal with attacks against Jesus' divine and human natures, and warn against false teachers. The third letter condemns a church leader who is opposing John's authority.

The writer does not identify himself, but the writing style and wording – especially in 1 John – are similar to that of the fourth Gospel, also an anonymous work but usually attributed to the apostle John. Church leaders in the second century quoted from the letters and said John wrote them late in life – at Ephesus.

Peter... has left one acknowledged epistle, and, it may be, a second one, for it is doubted.

ORIGEN, CHRISTIAN THEOLOGIAN, THIRD CENTURY AD

A sixth-century Byzantine mosaic of the apostle Peter.

LETTER TO THE HEBREWS

Hebrews was once attributed to Paul, but it is so different from Paul's authentic letters that it is now generally considered non-Pauline. However, it does seem to have been written for general distribution, putting it into a class with the General Letters. Although it is called "Letter to the Hebrews", it is not a true letter, lacking most of the attributes of a letter. Rather it is a formal tract written in highly polished Greek, which promotes the Christian way of life and exalts Jesus as the great high priest who offers himself as a sacrifice to his people. It is, therefore, not even written to Hebrews, but to Christians, albeit Christians familiar with the Jewish liturgy or attracted by the values of the Jewish cult.

There is no way to determine either the author of this work or its intended readers. All we can surmise is that the author was a Christian who was well acquainted with both the Greek Septuagint and Hebrew versions of Jewish Scripture. He probably wrote the "letter" between AD 60 and 90.

Letter of Jude

In this 25-verse letter, the writer identifies himself as "Jude, a servant of Jesus Christ and brother of James" (Jude 1). Some scholars say Jude was a brother of Jesus. That would explain why he mentioned James, the well-known brother of Jesus who led the Jerusalem church. The Gospels say Jesus had four brothers, including James and Judas (Jude).

The letter attacks a heretical teaching that says it is all right for Christians to sin, perhaps referring to a movement that emerged in the late first century. For this reason, some scholars suggest that a later respected church leader – also named Jude – wrote the letter.

Anticipating the End Time

APOCALYPTIC LITERATURE AND THE BOOK OF REVELATION

The final book of the New Testament is the Revelation to John, an apocalyptic work. The term "apocalyptic" (from the Greek *apocalypsis*, meaning "revelation") is generally applied to visionary writings that focus on the end time.

Generally, apocalypses were written during times of persecution but set in a past period of turmoil, such as the years of exile in Babylon. A typical apocalypse is narrated by a prominent biblical figure, such as Abraham or Elijah. The narrator is visited by an angel or some other spiritual being who presents visions of future events that often include otherworldly journeys or cosmic displays. In essence, the visions reveal that God is always in charge; even though bad times are approaching, good will triumph in the end.

Daniel, Enoch, and Mark

Chapters 7–12 of the book of Daniel constitute the first true apocalypse, including a series of visions and the appearance of an angel who predicts the future. There will be devastation and anguish exceeding any that has been known before. But deliverance will follow and even resurrection, for "Many of those who sleep in the dust of the earth shall awake, some to everlasting life, and some to shame and everlasting contempt" (Daniel 12:2).

Among the most fascinating extra-biblical apocalypses are those attributed to Enoch. According to the Bible, Enoch, the father of Methuselah, did not die. Rather, when he was 365 years old, "Enoch walked with God; then he was no more, because God took him" (Genesis 5:24). This mysterious statement led to many legends about Enoch, as well as three apocalyptic books. The first two are particularly interesting as they tell of Enoch's time in

> *The revelation of Jesus Christ, which God gave him to show his servants what must soon take place; he made it known by sending his angel to his servant John, who testified to the word of God and to the testimony of Jesus Christ, even to all that he saw.*
>
> REVELATION 1:1–2

INFLUENCES ON THE GENRE

The apocalyptic genre evolved slowly, possibly growing out of the prophetic tradition. Elements of the genre are found in Ezekiel and Zechariah. The book of Ezekiel is constructed around five visions that predict judgment and salvation. In the eight visions of Zechariah 1–6 the prophet describes supernatural phenomena that an angel then explains as bearing on future events.

This illustration from the tenth-century *Commentary on the Apocalypse of Beatus* shows a trumpet announcing the fall of Babylon/Rome.

heaven and focus on God's final judgment. Chapters 1–36 of 1 Enoch, known separately as *The Book of Watchers*, were probably written in the third century BC. They tell the story of the rebellion in heaven and the fall of the angels. Possibly dating to the first century AD, 2 Enoch tells of Enoch's travels through the heavens and his interview with the Lord in the Seventh Heaven, where he learns the secrets of creation and human history.

Even the Gospels have aspects of the apocalyptic. In chapter 13 of Mark's Gospel, Jesus warns his disciples of pain and persecutions to come, but assures them that he will come again to put all things right. The language in this section is also apocalyptic in tone, as Jesus speaks of the sun and moon going dark and the stars falling from the heavens just before he comes again.

The Revelation to John

The final book of the Bible gets its name from the opening verse: "The revelation of Jesus Christ" (Revelation 1:1). Although the word *apocalypsis* once meant simply "an unveiling", because of the earth-shattering events described in the book, it came to mean an extinction-level catastrophe.

The author of the book of Revelation identifies himself as a Christian named John, exiled to the small and rocky island of Patmos for preaching about Jesus. But which John? Justin Martyr, a second-century Christian writer, said the writer was the apostle John, one of Jesus' closest disciples and the presumed author of the Gospel of John and the three

letters of John. Within about 100 years, other church leaders began to challenge this answer, arguing that the book was nothing like John's other works.

Whoever the author was, Revelation was probably written in the final decade of the first century, when Emperor Domitian renewed the persecution of Christians, executing many and exiling others to penal colonies. The vexing symbolism in Revelation apparently allowed the writer to encourage the Christian churches without repercussions from Rome. The Christians understood the coded images, many of which were drawn from the Old Testament. But to Romans, it probably read like the fantasy of a lonely man with too much time on his hands.

So Revelation closes the book of the Bible – and human history. But it opens the door to a new age of peace in which God has defeated evil, and the faithful live with him forever.

The *Apocalypse of Peter*

Among the later apocalyptic writings, the *Apocalypse of Peter* was the most popular, possibly because it provided vivid details about the afterlife.

The longest section of the work, a tour of hell, traces 21 types of sinner and their appropriate punishments. For example, people who spoke against God were hung "by their tongues" over an "unquenchable fire". Murderers were cast into a place "full of evil, creeping things, and smitten by those beasts... and upon them were set worms like clouds of darkness".

This visionary book claims to be a revelation that the resurrected Jesus gave to the apostle Peter, but it was probably not written until long after Peter's death, possibly during the failed Jewish rebellion against Rome in AD 132–135. For a time it was considered for inclusion in the New Testament canon, and continued to be read by some in church into the fifth century.

Left: The *Apocalypse of Peter* features a graphic tour of hell, which may have inspired Dante's *Inferno* and this painting of hell in *The Garden of Earthly Delights* by Hieronymus Bosch (1450–1576).

Apostolic Fathers & Unwanted Gospels

APPROVED AND REJECTED

Who you know is not solely a modern concern. Even ancient Christians cared. In the late second century, the Christian writer Irenaeus boasted of his memories of the martyr Polycarp, who had known the apostle John and repeated his words to him, thus creating a direct link between Irenaeus, the apostles, and Jesus himself.

Since the seventeenth century, writers who knew someone who knew Jesus have been called apostolic fathers. This excludes Irenaeus, as he did not personally know an apostle, but only someone (Polycarp) who knew someone (John) who knew Jesus. But even such a tenuous link to Jesus seemed worth boasting about.

The apostolic fathers, then, were the elite of the primitive church and were influential in determining and recording which books and letters would later form part of the New Testament. Others had different views, and they produced their own Gospels, which the apostolic fathers and those with like views rejected.

Ignatius, bishop of Antioch, was martyred for his Christian faith.

St Polycarp, one of the apostolic fathers, and St Sebastian, an early martyr, destroy pagan idols in a Christian convert's home.

Someone Who Knew Someone Who Knew Jesus

In addition to Polycarp, the apostolic fathers include Clement I, a bishop of Rome who wrote a revered letter to the Corinthians (*1 Clement*), and Ignatius, bishop of Antioch, who, when thrown to wild beasts as a martyr, boasted: "I am God's wheat and I am being ground by the teeth of wild beasts to make a pure loaf for Christ."

Four others are included among the apostolic fathers for what they wrote. The anonymous author of *Clement's Second Letter* (*2 Clement*) – wrongly identified as Clement – wrote the first full Christian sermon to survive. The author of the *Epistle of Barnabas* (not the apostle, as once claimed) discusses the relationship between Judaism and Christianity. The authors of the *Didache* and the *Shepherd of Hermas* have much to say about second-century Christian life.

Knowledge of New Testament Books

By the time of the apostolic fathers, all the books of the New Testament had probably been written, but there was as yet no official canon (from the Greek word meaning "measuring rod", this word meant which books measured up to being included in God's divine word). One of the criteria for deciding on the books to be included, however, would be their use by Christian churches. We can glean much of what was being read in the second century from the apostolic fathers:

As children of the light of truth, flee from division and false teaching. Where the shepherd is, there follow like sheep.

IGNATIUS, BISHOP OF ANTIOCH

- Polycarp, in his *Letter to the Philippians*, urges the Philippians to study the letters Paul has written to them. Polycarp also quotes from Matthew, Luke, the letters of John, and 1 Peter.

- Ignatius, in his seven surviving letters, freely quotes from Paul's letters and infuses his Pauline thought with elements that are reminiscent of John.

- The *Epistle of Barnabas* is similar in tone to Hebrews, which the author must have read.

- The *Didache*, a church manual, seems to be an extension of concepts from Matthew.

- The *Shepherd of Hermas* echoes Matthew, Mark, John, Ephesians, and Revelation.

- *1 Clement* alludes to Matthew, Mark, Luke, Acts, Romans, 1 Corinthians, Galatians, Philippians, 1 Timothy, Titus, and 1 Peter.

- *2 Clement* cites two classes of writing in the church – the Bible and the Apostles – thus equating the Old Testament (the Bible) with the New (the Apostles).

What the Gnostics Taught

Not all early Christians shared the beliefs of the apostolic fathers. One dissident group, the Gnostics, drew their teachings from Judaism, Christianity, and Greek and Egyptian mythology. Gnostics did not always agree with each other, yet several non-traditional ideas repeatedly show up in their writings. They include:

- The Old Testament God, who created the world, is not the Supreme Being, but a lesser god; all he created – humans included – is evil.

- Jesus was a spirit being who only appeared human. He did not suffer pain, die on the cross, or rise from the dead.

- We are saved by spiritual knowledge. The ultimate God sent a redeemer to bring knowledge to the spirits trapped in human bodies. To find salvation and ascend to God's world of pure spirit, humans needed to receive this knowledge.

- There are three kinds of people: Those who are born with spiritual knowledge and can teach it; those who are capable of learning it; and those who are incapable of enlightenment – the vast majority.

UNWANTED GNOSTIC GOSPELS

The Gnostics, who appeared early in the history of Christianity, got their name from the Greek word *gnosis* ("knowledge") because they believed people were saved through secret knowledge, not faith in Jesus, and 1 Timothy 6:20 warns against them: "Avoid the profane chatter and contradictions of what is falsely called knowledge." Still, the movement grew and, in about AD 180, Irenaeus wrote *Against the Heresies*, which sharply condemned Gnosticism.

For centuries almost everything known about the Gnostics came from the writings of Irenaeus. Then, in 1945, two brothers who were digging near the Egyptian town of Nag Hammadi discovered a clay jar containing a dozen books. The books contain fourth-century Egyptian translations of 52 second-century Greek manuscripts. About half of the texts are apocalypses, or revelations – in line with the gnostic emphasis on revealed knowledge. Still others are wisdom writings, doctrinal teachings, prayers, hymns, re-workings of Old Testament stories, and Gospels.

This gnostic amulet from the late Byzantine period depicts the sacrifice of Isaac. Such amulets were believed to have magical powers.

THE GOSPEL OF THOMAS

The most famous of the gnostic writings is the Gospel of Thomas, which is not a traditional Gospel but a list of 114 sayings of Jesus. About half of these sayings are also found in the New Testament Gospels. Most of the others point towards gnostic ideas. For example, saying number 70 supports the gnostic idea that humans are saved by knowledge hidden within them: "If you bring forth what is within you, what you bring forth will save you." Scholars disagree over whether these sayings came from first-century witnesses or were written in the second or third century, during the peak of gnostic influence.

Fragment of the Gospel of Thomas.

Early Christian Worship

THE WORD AND THE EUCHARIST

The earliest Christians were also Jews, so they worshipped as the Jews did in the synagogues. At a typical synagogue service, it was the custom to read from the Pentateuch and the Prophets. A synagogue official would generally choose someone from the congregation to do a reading and the reader would give a talk, interpreting the passage he had just read. Christians would have followed this pattern strictly at first, later adding more specifically Christian prayers, blessings, and hymns.

Gathering Together on the Lord's Day

The earliest Christians attended synagogue but also gathered together – generally in each other's houses – to give thanks for Jesus and remember his breaking of bread at the Last Supper. This service of the Lord's Supper became known as the Eucharist, from the Greek word meaning "thanksgiving". Initially the word was used to describe only the prayers said at the service, but soon it became the name of the service itself.

At first, the breaking of bread took place at a full meal and Paul worried that some Christians ate too much while others did not get enough. Consequently, he advised them: "When you come together to eat, wait for one another. If you are hungry, eat at home, so that when you come together, it will not be for your condemnation" (1 Corinthians 11:33–34).

The *Didache*, a kind of church manual from the second century, instructs Christians to deal with their sins before coming to the Eucharist. "On every Lord's Day – his special day – come together and break bread and give thanks, first confessing your sins so that your sacrifice may be pure" (*Didache* 14:1).

The order of the Eucharist is more fully described by Justin Martyr, from Rome, in the mid second century:

On the day called Sunday there is a meeting in one place of those who live in cities or the country, and the memoirs of the apostles or the writings of the prophets are read as long as time permits. When the reader has finished, the president in a discourse urges and invites [those in attendance] to the imitation of those noble things. Then we all stand up and offer prayers.

This part of the Christian service, then, resembles synagogue services except that New Testament readings (the memoirs of the apostles) were given and then interpreted by the church president, not the reader.

After the president's homily, Justin tells us, bread and wine and water are brought out, prayers are said by the president, and the bread and wine are distributed to those present and taken out to others by deacons. The service takes place on Sunday because it is the day on which God began the creation and the day on which Jesus rose from the dead. In the beginning, Jewish Christians probably went to the synagogue on Saturday (the Jewish Sabbath) and then gathered for the Eucharist on Sunday, but by the mid second century they had combined the services into one on Sundays.

This early Christian wall painting from the catacomb of St Peter and Marcellinus shows a eucharistic love feast – a communal meal commemorating the Last Supper.

● SEE ALSO
JEWISH WORSHIP AND THE PSALMS,
PP. 14–15
MEDIEVAL WORSHIP, PP. 74–75

For the apostles in the memoirs composed by them, which are called Gospels, thus handed down what was commanded them: that Jesus taking bread and having given thanks said, "Do this for my memorial, this is my body..."

JUSTIN MARTYR, *APOLOGY* 1:85

Prayers, Hymns, and Other Matters

The prayers said at early Christian services were sometimes taken from the Gospels and Pauline letters. Paramount among them, of course, were the words Jesus spoke over the bread and the wine, as reported in 1 Corinthians 11:24–25. Another eucharistic prayer, found in the *Didache*, points to the coming kingdom of God: "As this broken bread was scattered upon the mountains, but was gathered together and became one, so let your church be gathered together from the ends of the earth."

Worshippers may also have recited the prayer that tells how Jesus emptied himself of Godhood for our sake, as found in Philippians 2:6–11. They certainly recited the Lord's Prayer, as found in Matthew 6:9–13, and they may have sung the hymns now found in Colossians 1:15–20, Ephesians 1:13–14, and 1 Timothy 3:16.

In the second century, worship services were long and included disconnected readings, but by the third century, they had been shortened. On feast days, the readings were chosen to fit the event being celebrated. For example, during the week before Easter, the readings came from Job because Job's suffering was seen in relation to Christ's, and on Easter Day, Jonah was read because Jonah's three days in the belly of the great fish were seen to predict Jesus' three days in a tomb. This was the start of liturgical reform, which continues today.

THE RITE OF BAPTISM

Only baptized men and women were allowed to partake of the Eucharist. From the early days, baptism incorporated the actions of John the Baptist and the words of Jesus. The *Didache* gives more precise instructions for baptisms, allowing variations to fit circumstances:

This is how to baptize: give public instruction on all these points and then "baptize" in running water, "in the name of the Father and of the Son and of the Holy Spirit". If you do not have running water, baptize in some other. If you cannot in cold, then in warm. If you have neither, then pour water on the head three times "in the name of the Father and of the Son and of the Holy Spirit". Before the baptism, moreover, the one who baptizes and the one being baptized must fast, and any others who can. And you must tell the one being baptized to fast for one or two days beforehand.

Detail from *Baptism of Cornelius by the Apostle Peter*, a relief from the so-called sarcophagus of the "miraculous source".

45

From Scroll to Codex

A New Format for Books

In Old Testament times most writing was done on papyrus. However, papyrus generally did not last very long and it was largely imported from Egypt, a land often at war with Israel. For a time leather was used, but it was too thick and cumbersome. Then, sometime before 500 BC, parchment was developed in Pergamum, a city in Asia Minor (now Turkey). Like leather, parchment was made from animal skins, but the process of preparing it produced a finer, more flexible medium for writing.

By the time of Jesus, parchment sheets were being bound together into books, or codices. Christians took to the codex, which soon replaced the scroll. Our oldest complete Bibles and the first ever study Bible were in codex form.

A Roman wax tablet.

Making Parchment

Parchment could be made from the skins of almost any animal – such as goat, deer, rabbit, or squirrel – but the best quality was obtained from calfskin. Called vellum, this fine parchment was used for precious manuscripts throughout the Middle Ages.

Parchment was made in four major steps: (1) The skin was taken from the animal and carefully cleaned and soaked to loosen the hair. (2) A worker used a blunt two-handled curved knife to scrape the hair and any residue of flesh off the skin. (3) The skin was rinsed and then stretched tightly over a wooden frame. (4) The skin was scraped again on both sides to reduce it to the desired thinness, then removed from the frame and rolled up. Just before use it was trimmed to size and buffed with pumice to whiten its surface.

After use, parchment could be scraped down and used again. Because it was supple, it was easily folded. This made it ideal for use in a new form of manuscript, which was made up of smaller pages that were bound together – in place of single rolled scrolls. This new form was the codex, or the book as we know it.

In a re-enactment of parchment making, a craftsman stretches a hide over a fire to dry it.

Making Books

This new book form was developed from a much more primitive writing medium called the caudex (later codex) from the Latin word *caudeus*, meaning "wooden". The original codex consisted of wooden boards that were hollowed out on one flat surface, filled with wax, and tied together to form a crude notebook. The Romans wrote in the soft wax with the pointed end of a metal stylus and erased texts with the blunt end.

In time, papyrus or parchment sheets were used instead of the cumbersome boards. At first, several sheets were stacked and then folded in half to form a simple pamphlet. Later, writers began to stitch together a number of pamphlets along their folds, creating a book with more pages – a codex. According to tradition, Mark first recorded his Gospel in a kind of codex, and other Christian writers followed suit. Out of about 870 surviving codices from these times, all but 14 contain Christian writings.

> *When you come, bring the cloak that I left with Carpus at Troas, also the books, and above all the parchments.*
>
> 2 TIMOTHY 4:13

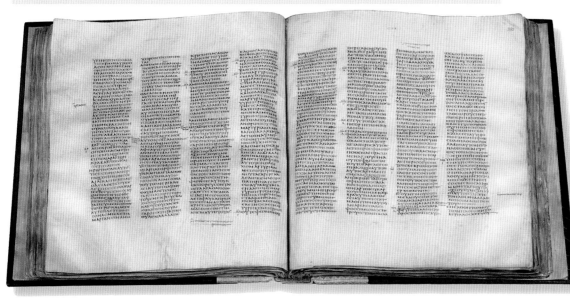

Two pages from the *Codex Sinaiticus*, one of the oldest surviving Bibles.

Making Collections and Complete Bibles

When the Gospels were first written, they were mainly used by the communities in which they were written. But when they proved to be of value to all Christians, they began to be bound together and circulated in the form of codices, or books. The same is true of Paul's letters.

No one knows when the Old and New Testaments were first combined and copied into a single volume, but the two oldest surviving (almost) complete Bibles were created in the mid fourth century. Known today as the *Codex* *Vaticanus* and the *Codex Sinaiticus*, they contain most of the text of the Septuagint (the first Greek translation of the Hebrew Bible), including the Apocrypha, though the *Codex Vaticanus* (now in Rome) is missing the books of the Maccabees. In addition, both codices contain all 27 books of the New Testament. The *Codex Sinaiticus* (discovered in 1844 at St Catherine's Monastery in Sinai, Egypt) also includes the *Epistle of Barnabas* and the *Shepherd of Hermas*. Because of their antiquity and near completeness, these two codices are of invaluable help to biblical scholars today.

THE FIRST STUDY BIBLE

The first-known study Bible, completed in about AD 245, brought together six versions of the Old Testament (but not the New) in side-by-side columns. This allowed readers to compare one version of a passage to another. The six-column format earned the work its name: *Hexapla* (Greek for "sixfold").

The *Hexapla* was created by Origen, one of the greatest writers of the early church. As a lifelong student of the Bible, Origen undertook the project to help him understand the Old Testament of which there were many versions, including Hebrew versions that contained passages that others did not have. There were also many Greek translations of the Hebrew Scriptures, including several variations of the Septuagint.

Origen decided to put the standard Hebrew text and five Greek translations in parallel columns for easier study. The fifth column was reserved for the Septuagint, which Origen himself painstakingly revised, attempting to reconcile the different versions.

Origen's manuscripts were lost in the early 600s and no complete copy was ever made. Some people did, however, copy parts of it, and fragments of those copies survive.

Origen in a 1584 engraving.

Quest for a Christian Bible

Various Approaches to Shaping It

For the first 100 years after Jesus, Christians regarded the books of the Hebrew Bible as their only Holy Scriptures, as they pointed to the coming of Jesus, their Saviour. Although they made frequent use of the Gospels and Pauline letters in teaching and worship, there was no official group of Christian writings. Meanwhile, Christians were often persecuted and their texts burned, and divergent versions of Christian belief emerged. Recognizing the need for an official body of Christian writings, various Christian leaders and scholars had differing ideas about what the collection should contain. Some wished to limit or even expurgate the Christian Scriptures, others wished to conflate them, while still others preferred to leave them open-ended. Ideas were bandied about for more than 200 years, and it was only when the new emperor Constantine took a personal interest in the Christian Bible that serious efforts were made to resolve the issue.

Marcion's New Testament

The first-known list of "acceptable" Christian writings was put together in about AD 140 by Marcion, a Gnostic, who taught that there were two gods: the lesser, evil, creator god of the Hebrew Scriptures and the loving God revealed by Jesus Christ – and Paul. Consequently, Marcion rejected the entire Old Testament, arguing that the spiritual heroes and prophets in those books had been deceived by the evil creator god. In addition, many Christian writers, he held, had also been misled by these Hebrew texts and so the entire body of Christian writings had to be cleansed. Marcion subsequently produced his own bowdlerized version of the New Testament, which was, essentially, a heavily edited version of 10 Pauline letters and Luke's Gospel (which had been written basically for non-Jewish Christians). Holding that everything physical was created by the evil god, Marcion insisted that because Jesus was not really human, but only appeared to be human, he could not be touched by anything physical, or human, because it was evil. Consequently, Marcion carefully excised any mention of Jesus' humanity, notably deleting all references to Jesus taking human form and suffering for the sins of humanity. Although considered heretical today, Marcion's Bible was widely accepted in his time.

Tatian's Four-in-One Gospel

By AD 150, all four Gospels were circulating throughout the church, but coping with four versions of the story of Jesus was confusing, with details in one Gospel occasionally seeming to clash with details in another. In about 170 a gnostic Christian teacher named Tatian decided to resolve the confusion. His *Diatessaron* blended the four Gospels along with material from the oral tradition. This masterfully woven Gospel remained the preferred version for many Syrian churches until the early 400s, when a Syrian bishop declared Tatian a heretic and ordered the churches to use other Gospel translations.

This parchment fragment, found at Dura-Europos, Syria, may be a part of a Gospel, like Tatian's, that blends the Gospels of Matthew, Mark, Luke, and John.

Gravitating towards the Most Used

None of the above approaches was universally accepted. Generally, individual congregations chose their own texts for use in worship services. The stories and letters they read most often were generally the most traditional, useful, and dear to the hearts of believers. With this in mind, the theologian Origen took a poll of what the various congregations were using. From his findings he compiled a three-part list of acceptable, questionable, and unreliable books. On his list of acceptable books were the four Gospels, thirteen letters of Paul, Acts of the Apostles, 1 Peter, 1 John, and Revelation. On his questionable list were Hebrews, James, 2 Peter, 2 and 3 John, and Jude. On his list of unreliable books were the Gospel of Thomas, the Gospel of the Egyptians, and the Gospel of Matthias.

It is clearly proved that neither the prophets nor the apostles did ever name another God, or call him Lord, except the true and only God.

IRENAEUS, *AGAINST HERESIES*

MONTANUS'S NEVER-ENDING BIBLE

Near the end of the second century, a cult leader named Montanus opted for an open-ended New Testament. A priest from a pagan ecstasy cult in what is now Turkey, Montanus converted to Christianity, then started a prophecy movement, claiming to receive messages directly from God. Montanus convinced many that he and his followers were instruments of the outpouring of the Holy Spirit predicted by John: "When the Spirit of truth comes, he will guide you into all the truth… and he will declare to you the things that are to come" (John 16:13). The Montanus movement, which continued for several centuries, urged Christians to keep the canon of Scripture open because God keeps the channel of revelation open through the continuing ministry of prophets. The church eventually responded by arguing that all the revelations necessary for salvation are contained in the writings from the apostles.

Before converting to Christianity, Montanus, who advocated an open-ended New Testament, was a priest of a pagan ecstasy cult, who would have offered sacrifices to the goddess Cybele and other deities, as does the priest in this Roman sandstone relief.

Eusebius and the Emperor
● ●

The periods of intermittent Christian persecutions ended in AD 312, when Constantine fought under the sign of Christ's cross and became emperor of the West. After signing the Edict of Milan the following year, legitimizing and even favouring Christianity, Constantine sent to Eusebius, the bishop of Caesarea, Palestine, and requisitioned 50 copies of the Christian Bible for churches he planned to build. Having to decide which books he would include in the emperor's Bibles, Eusebius compiled a three-part list, as Origen had done, and ended up with nearly the same list of approved books, though he seemed uncertain about Revelation, which he approved only "if it seems desirable". Unfortunately, none of these imperial Bibles survives, but a single complete Bible from that time does. The *Codex Sinaiticus* (at St Catherine's Monastery, Sinai, Egypt) has all of the New Testament books plus the *Letter of Barnabas* and the *Shepherd of Hermas*.

Emperor Constantine, seen here with his mother Helena, requisitioned 50 Christian Bibles, prompting Christian leaders to decide quickly what books the New Testament should include.

Settling the New Testament

ESTABLISHING A 27-BOOK CANON

The first time the exact 27 books of the New Testament were listed anywhere was in an Easter letter by an Egyptian bishop some 70 years old. In AD 367 Bishop Athanasius of Alexandria wrote his annual Easter letter to churches in his jurisdiction, to teach and encourage the believers. In this memorable letter Athanasius, after expressing concern that heretics were making use of unauthoritative texts to spread evil doctrines, declared the need to "clearly identify what books have been received by us through tradition as belonging to the canon, and which we believe to be divine". The bishop then listed the Old Testament books, followed by the New Testament books, from Matthew to Revelation. In conclusion, Athanasius wrote: "These are the fountains of salvation, that they who thirst may be satisfied with the living words they contain. In these alone is proclaimed the doctrine of godliness. Let no one add to or take anything from them."

Affirming Athanasius's Canon

Athanasius was not expressing just his personal opinion in his pastoral letter. He was reporting the prevailing attitude of the church. Indeed, his assessment was confirmed when church leaders adopted his canon at several North African conferences: in Hippo in 393, at Carthage in 397, and – in response to some leaders calling for the removal of Hebrews, James, and Jude from the canon – at Carthage a second time in 419.

It was near the end of a long and stormy career (fighting popular heresies) that Athanasius, shown above in the painting by Francesco Solimena (1657–1747), presented his comments on the New Testament canon. He was also the first to use the word "canon" to describe the contents of the Bible. There had been, of course, no formal criteria for determining the contents of the biblical canon – hence the difficulty at arriving at one. Generally, though, scholars deduce that there were three major requirements: (1) the book had been written by an apostle or an apostle's close associate; (2) it was in line with traditional Christian teaching; and (3) it had been widely used in churches and recognized as authoritative.

> *All scripture is inspired by God, and is useful for teaching, for reproof, for correction, and for training in righteousness.*
>
> **2 TIMOTHY 3:16**

For most Christians, the question of the New Testament had been settled. The 27 books were almost universally accepted as the second part of the Bible. But lingering debate persisted, and there has never been complete agreement. Several decades later, the *Codex Alexandrinus*, a copy of the Bible from Alexandria, Egypt, included two letters written by Clement, a church leader from the late first century. Athanasius had never mentioned these letters, but they had been included in the New Testament in this copy of the Bible. Meanwhile, Syrian Christians continued using the *Diatessaron* – the four Gospels as Tatian had blended them together in the second century – well into the 400s (and beyond in many churches). Even today, some churches in eastern Syria exclude 2 Peter, 2 and 3 John, Jude, and Revelation. The Ethiopian Church, on the other hand, adds to the canon; it has 38 books instead of 27.

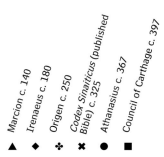

	Marcion c. 140 ▲	Irenaeus c. 180 ◆	Origen c. 250 ✣	Codex Sinaiticus (published Bible) c. 325 ✗	Athanasius c. 367 ●	Council of Carthage c. 397 ■
MATTHEW		◆	✣	✗	●	■
MARK		◆	✣	✗	●	■
LUKE	▲	◆	✣	✗	●	■
JOHN		◆	✣	✗	●	■
ACTS		◆	✣	✗	●	■
ROMANS	▲	◆	✣	✗	●	■
1 & 2 CORINTHIANS	▲	◆	✣	✗	●	■
GALATIANS	▲	◆	✣	✗	●	■
EPHESIANS	▲	◆	✣	✗	●	■
PHILIPPIANS	▲	◆	✣	✗	●	■
COLOSSIANS	▲	◆	✣	✗	●	■
1 & 2 THESSALONIANS	▲	◆	✣	✗	●	■
1 & 2 TIMOTHY		◆	✣	✗	●	■
TITUS		◆	✣	✗	●	■
PHILEMON	▲	◆	✣	✗	●	■
HEBREWS				✗	●	■
JAMES				✗	●	■
1 PETER				✗	●	■
2 PETER		◆	✣	✗	●	■
1 JOHN		◆	✣	✗	●	■
2 JOHN		◆		✗	●	■
3 JOHN				✗	●	■
JUDE				✗	●	■
REVELATION		◆	✣	✗	●	■
SHEPHERD OF HERMAS		◆		✗		
EPISTLE OF BARNABAS		◆		✗		

A page from the fifth-century Greek *Codex Alexandrinus*.

Contenders for the New Testament

Early church scholars, councils and ancient editions of the Bible did not always agree on which books Christians should revere. Egyptian bishop Athanasius, in an Easter letter to his churches in AD 367, was the first person in history known to list the 27 books that Christians today call the New Testament. For most Christians, the issue was settled 30 years later at the Council of Carthage, although some disagreement lingered. The chart shows which books were included in various early lists. All but the last two of the books shown in this table (right) were eventually included in the New Testament.

"Almost" Scriptures and More

NON-CANONICAL BOOKS AND A FEW GOOD READS

In the opinion of some early church leaders, not all the books that belonged in the New Testament were there. These same leaders would probably have agreed that others, though widely read, were best left out. Although many Christian writings failed to make the final cut for the New Testament, some were serious contenders. Irenaeus, Tertullian, Origen, and other church leaders insisted that at least four books – all by apostolic fathers – deserved inclusion in the Bible. They were the *Shepherd of Hermas*, the *Didache*, and two notable letters. Other books lost out because they had only their popularity to recommend them; they were really good reads, including dubious tales of Jesus' infancy and a tumultuous tale of Paul and a female disciple.

Shepherd of Hermas

Written in the mid second century, *Shepherd of Hermas* dealt with a wide range of moral issues that called believers to holy living and self-control. In the book, a celestial shepherd (presumably an angel) gives spiritual advice to Hermas, a former slave turned businessman. The book is divided into three sections: visions, sermons, and parables. The visions resemble the dozens of apocalypses written in this era. The sermons and parables cover such topics as sexual purity, repentance, patience, and anger. The book also settles some controversies. For example, when Hermas asks if sins committed after baptism can be forgiven, the shepherd says that forgiveness after baptism is available, but only once and for a limited time.

Elsewhere, the messenger reveals that each of us is accompanied by an angel of righteousness and an angel of wickedness. We should heed the advice of the righteous angel and repel the angel of wickedness.

Didache

"The Teaching of the Twelve Apostles" is a slim handbook for training converts in basic Christian beliefs, behaviour, and worship rituals. It is generally referred to as the *Didache* (Greek for "teaching").

The *Didache* was probably written late first or early second century, when Christians and Jews were trying to distance themselves from one another. For example, Christians are told to fast and pray, as the Jews do, but to fast on different days and say the Lord's Prayer.

The *Didache* also offers advice about appropriate Christian behaviour, baptism, and Sunday worship. Sometimes its tone is gentle: "If you can bear the Lord's full yoke, you will be perfect, but if you cannot, then do what you can."

In this fourteenth-century painting, *Annunciation to the Shepherds*, angels announce the birth of Jesus. The *Shepherd of Hermas* was a book of advice given to a shepherd by a celestial messenger, probably an angel.

Two Letters

Two of the "almost" scriptures were letters written in the last years of the first century. Though both letters fail to identify their authors, one is generally attributed to Clement, bishop of Rome, and the other (more dubiously) to Barnabas, one of Paul's associates.

In *1 Clement*, the writer responds to appeals for help from the Christians in Corinth, who are again mired in power struggles. The letter advises hospitality, faith, and humility.

The *Epistle of Barnabas* discusses how Christians fit into God's covenant with the Jews and advocates proper Christian behaviour. It also holds that the hidden (allegorical) meanings of Old Testament passages are more reliable than obvious, literal meanings.

A man of small stature with a bald head and crooked legs, in a good state of body, with eyebrows meeting and a nose somewhat hooked, full of friendliness.

ACTS OF PAUL AND THECLA — THE ONLY KNOWN DESCRIPTION OF PAUL

Popular Infancy Gospels

By the end of the first century, almost everyone who had ever seen Jesus was dead, but Christians wanted to hear more about Jesus' life than the Gospels told them. They especially wanted to know about Jesus' childhood. In response, dozens of infancy Gospels appeared, filled with stories both factual and fanciful. Most notable was the *Infancy Gospel of Thomas*, a short collection of miracles Jesus supposedly performed between the ages of five and twelve. The "Gospel" claims to have been written by a Jew named Thomas. The book does not always portray Jesus as saintly. Instead, it shows his transformation from an immature and vindictive boy who used his supernatural powers for revenge to a compassionate adolescent who started using his powers to help others.

For example, when the five-year-old Jesus was playfully making little pools of water in the mud, another boy used a willow branch to drain the pools. Angered by this Jesus told the boy, "Behold, even now you will be dried up." And the boy withered and died.

Later, however, when a playmate fell from a roof, Jesus raised him from the dead. And when Joseph cut a beam too short for a couch he was making, Jesus stretched the beam.

In a popular story, Thecla delivers a city from plague through her prayers, as shown above in a detail from a painting by Giovanni Battista Tiepolo (1696–1770).

Dubious Acts of the Apostles

Acts of John tells of the apostle John's perilous travels as he spread the good news far and wide. Surviving storms, earthquakes, and imprisonments, John preached and worked miracles in Jesus' name. While staying at an inn one night, John ordered the bed bugs out of his room. "O bugs," John said, "leave your abode for this night and remain quiet in one place." The next morning John found a throng of bugs waiting outside his door. He told them that since they had behaved, they could go home. They skittered back into the mattress and disappeared.

Acts of Paul and Thecla is a story about an 18-year-old woman who broke off her engagement after hearing Paul preach about celibacy. Furious, Thecla's mother cried out for her daughter to be burnt alive. Tied to a pyre, Thecla escaped after a cloudburst washed out the fire. Thecla followed Paul on a missionary journey, miraculously surviving more attempts on her life. Later, she lived quietly and simply, but became famous for healing the sick.

Left: Clement, bishop of Rome, the supposed author of *1 Clement*, has a vision of the Trinity in this painting by Giovanni Battista Tiepolo.

Ways of Reading the Bible

INTERPRETING THE WORD OF GOD

Although Jews probably discussed the meaning of their Scriptures since the first scroll was copied, their views were passed down only by word of mouth. Some biblical texts, however, function as commentaries. For example, when the author of Chronicles rewrote Samuel and Kings, he cleaned up the images of David and Solomon. In doing so he was subtly commenting on the earlier books, which show those kings warts and all. Similarly, the Septuagint was a kind of commentary, as it used words of a different language – Greek – to interpret the Hebrew Scriptures for readers who did not understand Hebrew. Around the time of Jesus, though, formal biblical commentaries began to appear – and later flourished.

The Essenes

In the first centuries BC and AD the Essenes, a community of Hebrew men who lived in the desert, may have written the first true biblical commentaries, called *pesharim* in Hebrew. In these scrolls the Essenes typically quoted a biblical passage, then wrote an interpretation, often relating it to their own community, the messiah, or the end of time. The pesharim were not known outside the Essene community of Qumran until they were discovered in the 1940s along with other ancient scrolls in caves near the Dead Sea.

Above: Philo of Alexandria in a 1584 engraving by Thevet.

Philo of Alexandria

The first major commentator on the Bible was Philo of Alexandria, Egypt, who wrote in the first half of the first century AD. Philo's biblical commentaries fall into three groups:

1. Allegorical, or symbolic, interpretations of the first 17 chapters of Genesis in terms of morality and the quest of the soul for God.
2. Explanations of the Jewish laws. Although Philo interprets the laws symbolically, he also insists on their literal observance. For example, he concedes that circumcision is a symbol of abandoning things of the flesh, but insists upon it being done.
3. Questions and answers about passages from Genesis and Exodus. Philo generally answers these questions by first giving a literal explanation, and then a symbolic one.

New Testament Writers Interpret the Bible

About the time of Philo's death in AD 50, New Testament writers were beginning to work. The book of Hebrews, which may have been influenced by Philo, cites Old Testament passages and then comments on them in the light of Jesus. The Gospels, too, show how Jesus fulfilled the Hebrew Scriptures. Matthew, in particular, constantly refers to events in Jesus' ministry as in accordance with the prophets, and in the narrative of the holy innocents and the flight to Egypt, seems to parallel the infant Jesus with Moses. Paul sees the mothers of Abraham's two children as the mothers of the two covenants: Hagar represents the Old Testament and Sarah the New (Galatians 4:21–31).

This type of reading is now called typology, as the Old Testament person or event is seen as a "type" of Christ or something associated with him. For example, the passage through the Red Sea is a "type" of baptism. Later Christian commentators continued to search for "types", but when they wanted to explain obscure biblical passages or apply them to their own time they often turned, as Philo had, to allegory.

Allegorical Interpretations – from Alexandria

Allegory is a kind of extended metaphor in which an event is given a meaning beyond the obvious. Not surprisingly, allegorical interpretations of Scripture grew strongest in Alexandria, Philo's old home. Their most ardent adherent was Origen, the writer who had produced the *Hexapla*, or first study Bible.

In his attempts to interpret Scripture, Origen looked for three basic levels of meaning: (1) the literal, or historical, meaning (the least important); (2) the moral significance (what it means for us); and (3) the symbolic meaning, which he arrived at through the use of allegory. Origen's methods were adopted by others, who are said to be of the School of Alexandria.

While Origen's interpretations could be effective, some were overly elaborate. In the account of Jesus feeding the 5,000, Jesus commands that the people "sit down in groups on the green grass. So they sat down

SEE ALSO
SCHOLARS LOOK AT THE BIBLE, PP. 76–77
DIGGING UP THE PAST, PP. 108–109
BIBLICAL CRITICISM, PP. 114–15

The scriptures were composed by the spirit of God and... have not only a meaning that is manifest, but also another that is hidden as far as most people are concerned.

ORIGEN, *DE PRINCIPIIS*

The port of Alexandria, Egypt, as it appears today.

in groups of hundreds and of fifties" (Mark 6:39–40). Origen comments that the grass here represents the flesh and that the people sit on the grass in order to humble the flesh and prepare themselves to eat the loaves Jesus has blessed. They are broken into groups because not everyone is equally nourished by the words they hear. As to the numbers, 100 is a sacred number, representing completeness, while 50 symbolizes the forgiveness of sins.

A More Tempered Approach – from Antioch

In the third century, sharply criticizing the excesses of allegorical readings, writers, centred in Antioch, Syria, began writing more conservatively. Although they believed in multiple meanings, they insisted on keeping the text as written as the primary focus.

In the fourth century, one member of this School of Antioch, Diodore of Tarsus, took pains to establish the historical circumstances in which the biblical books were written. Only when he had done so did Diodore look for a higher meaning, which he insisted must be rooted in the text and not be a figment of the interpreter's imagination.

The School of Antioch all but disappeared by the end of the fifth century, while the allegorists remained strong. However, the influence of the Antiochenes may be seen in the more tempered use of allegory by later writers, including Jerome and Augustine.

Origen related the storm that struck the apostles' fishing boat to the daily conflicts we all face. Jesus allowed the storm to hit the boat to teach the apostles a lesson, but then he stilled the waters, as seen in this painting by James Tissot.

From Heretic to Saint

AUGUSTINE DISCOVERS THE BIBLE

The African bishop Augustine started out as a sinful young man who disdained the Bible. He ended as a saint and the greatest theologian of the Western Church, whose many writings are rooted in Scripture – including *City of God*, his monumental defence of Christianity. Once converted to Christianity, Augustine loved God with a passion, as can be seen in his emotionally charged autobiography, *Confessions*, and he spent the rest of his life making the messages of the Bible clear to the people in his care.

Pagan and Heretic

Augustine was born in 354 in the North African town of Thagaste (now Souk-Ahras, Algeria). His father was a pagan and his mother a Christian.

Although his mother urged him to become a Christian and constantly prayed for his conversion, Augustine preferred to lead a life of pleasure. At 17 he began a 15-year affair with a woman and fathered an illegitimate son. When he was 18, he felt spiritual stirrings and tried reading the Bible (in a poor Latin translation), but found its literary style distasteful.

Instead of becoming a Christian, Augustine fell in with a group of Manichees, followers of the Persian heretic Mani, who disdained the Old Testament and believed in a cosmos made up of two battling kingdoms, one of darkness and the other of light. Augustine remained with this group for about 10 years. In that time he left his mistress, expecting to get married, but then took up with another woman, and never married.

St Ambrose (339–397).

The Christian quarter in Hippo Regius.

The Lure of the Bible

Growing disillusioned with the Manichees, Augustine began to be swayed by sermons preached by Ambrose, the Christian bishop of Milan, where Augustine was teaching. Ambrose's allegorical readings of Scripture made Augustine realize that the Bible had merit after all. Slowly Augustine leaned towards Christianity.

Then, one July day in 386, Augustine tells us in his *Confessions*, he was thinking things over in a garden when he heard a child's voice chanting, "Take up and read, take up and read." He decided this was a message from heaven, so he picked up a copy of Paul's letters, opened it, and read: "Let us live honourably as in the day, not in revelling and drunkenness, not in debauchery and licentiousness, not in quarrelling and jealousy. Instead, put on the Lord Jesus Christ, and make no provision for the flesh, to gratify its desires" (Romans 13:13–14). Augustine was instantly converted and was baptized by Ambrose in 387.

After his mother died later that year Augustine returned to his home town, Thagaste, where he

Let Thy scriptures be my chaste delights. Neither let me be deceived in them, nor deceive out of them.

AUGUSTINE, *CONFESSIONS*

● SEE ALSO
WAYS OF READING THE BIBLE, PP. 54–55
JEROME, PP. 58–59

RULES FOR INTERPRETING SCRIPTURE

In *On Christian Doctrine*, Augustine laid down rules for interpreting Scripture that are still valid:

- Apply Hebrew and Greek scholarship, which are essential to interpreting the figurative language of Scripture.

- Become acquainted with everything to do with the Holy Land – its geography, natural history, music, chronology, and dialects. Also study the science of numbers and the writings of the ancient philosophers.

- Remember that Scripture is designed to have more than one interpretation.

- Interpret obscure passages by the light of passages that are understood. This is preferable to interpreting by reason.

Finally, Augustine held that the spirit and intent of the interpreter is more important than verbal accuracy and critical acumen. Mistaken interpretations are not necessarily bad. If a mistaken interpretation tends to build up love, which is the end of the commandment, the interpreter goes astray in much the same way as a man who, by mistake, quits the high road, but yet reaches, through the fields, the same place to which the road leads.

organized a group of laymen into a kind of monastic community. While visiting the nearby coastal town of Hippo Regius in 391, he was mobbed by people who wanted him to be their bishop. He was ordained a priest more or less against his will. In 395 he was named bishop of Hippo, where he remained, writing, fighting heresies, and living in community with his clergy until his death in 430.

Augustine and the Bible

During his 35 years as bishop of Hippo, Augustine wrote a vast number of books, letters, and sermons. Chief among his works on Scripture itself are *A Harmony of the Evangelists*, which lays down principles for dealing with the differences among the Synoptic Gospels (Matthew, Mark, and Luke), *On Christian Doctrine*, which gives guidelines for interpreting Scripture, *Tractates on John's Gospel*, and *Homilies on the Psalms*.

Unlike his contemporary Jerome, who took a scholarly approach to Scripture, Augustine designed his biblical commentaries to awaken the understanding of the people of his diocese. Consequently, he sacrificed literary style, which he admired, for clarity, using vivid everyday language that was aglow with fervent love.

In his interpretations of Scripture, Augustine followed Origen and others of the School of Alexandria in stressing the spiritual sense rather than the literal. However, he respected the literal meaning and was attentive to the text and the historical context in which it was written. For example, he held that the Gospels often report Jesus' words only in a general way, reflecting the broad sense of what Jesus said rather than his exact words.

For Augustine, the Bible speaks not only of promise and fulfilment in the person of Jesus, but gives literal or figurative answers to the basic questions of humanity. He held that God gave us the Scriptures to incite us to a double love of God and neighbour – the goal of every soul's journey. Even so, Augustine realized that the complexities and ambiguities of human language make it difficult to interpret Scripture, and he advised others to take particular care in doing so.

St Augustine by Justus van Gent.

Writing Down the Oral Law

RECORDING ANCIENT JEWISH TRADITIONS

Not all the religious laws the Jews live by are written in the Jewish Bible. Laws passed on by word of mouth, which were also believed to have come from God, are seen to carry the same authority as the Bible. When God delivered the law to Moses – the laws preserved in the first five books of the Bible – God gave added instructions that Moses did not write down. For example, God told Moses that the people should not work on the Sabbath. Moses put this in the written law. But Jewish teachers say that God also clarified for Moses what constituted work – such as drawing drinking water from a well. Over the centuries, this oral law expanded as new generations of Jewish religious leaders sought to interpret and apply the principles of God's laws to the ever-changing world. The oral law needed to be written down and the Bible itself needed to be standardized and clarified for later generations.

A page from the Mishnah dating from the eleventh or twelfth century.

Jewish men meet to study Scripture and the Talmud.

Second to the Bible for Jews

By the end of the second century AD the oral traditions had become so complex that many rabbis started making notes to help them remember – lest some of the oral laws be lost. In about AD 200, Rabbi Judah ha-Nasi decided to take the next logical step and put the oral law in writing. Assisted by teams of rabbis, he produced a document that Jews consider second only to the Bible in importance.

This document is the Mishnah, from a Hebrew word that meant "to recite", and later "to teach". A massive compilation, the Mishnah contains centuries of interpretation, from the earliest oral laws to the most recent.

The Mishnah is divided into six major sections, covering a wide range of Jewish life:

- "Seeds", which deals mainly with agriculture.
- "Appointed Seasons", which discusses Sabbath observation, religious festivals, and fast days.
- "Women", which covers laws affecting marriage, divorce, and other aspects of family life.
- "Damages", which covers civil and criminal laws, idolatry, and ethics.
- "Holy Things", which covers worship rituals.
- "Cleanliness", which focuses on laws of ritual purity.

The Talmud's Law and Lore

Jewish scholars continued discussing the law and they wrote down these discussions, along with biblical commentaries, stories by or about rabbis, teachings about demons, medical advice, science, history, legends, and rulings about religious matters handed down by the Jewish council.

In time, these wide-ranging discussions were collected into a massive work known as the Gemara, which was in turn combined with the Mishnah to form the Talmud. (Both "Talmud" and "Gemara" are from words that mean "study" or "learn".)

There are two versions of the Talmud, one from the region just north of Jerusalem and one from Mesopotamia, where many Jews had stayed after the Babylonian exile. The Jerusalem, or Palestinian, Talmud, was finished in about AD 450.

SEE ALSO
SETTLING THE JEWISH BIBLE,
PP. 26–27

A man should revere his father and mother as he reveres God, for all three are partners in him.
RABBI JUDAH HA-NASI

The Babylonian Talmud, which is about three times longer, was finished about a century later, and became the more widely accepted version.

Throughout the last 15 centuries, the Talmud has been a source of insight for Jews devoted to studying God's law and applying it to their lives. It is regarded by many as a vital and authoritative guide for living the Jewish life.

Clarifying the Hebrew Scriptures

Having recorded the oral law, Jews also needed to standardize the Bible itself. Until the second century AD, when the Jewish canon was closed, biblical texts had been in flux. Some books were still being given final shape. For example, the book of Jeremiah existed in two versions, one much longer than the other. But then everything changed. Scribes were charged with copying the texts with extreme accuracy. Because the Jews were widely dispersed around the Mediterranean at the time, they must have felt the need for a standardized text that would unify them in their beliefs, and so, over the next few centuries, scholars worked hard to produce one. One rabbi warned his scribes that to eliminate or add a single letter to the text would destroy the world.

Then, between AD 500 and 1000, a special group of scribes developed an official Hebrew text of the Old Testament. Because they were considered masters of the *masorah* ("what has been handed down"), they were called the Masoretes. The Masoretes also divided the biblical texts into paragraphs, marked passages to be used for synagogue readings, and made notes of possible textual errors, letting readers decide for themselves the correct reading. The Masoretic text is the standard Hebrew text of the Bible today.

Vowel Markings

The words the Masoretes worked so hard to preserve consisted of consonants only. In Hebrew, vowels were not written. Readers had to supply the vowels themselves, and this could be tricky because words using the same sequence of consonants may represent different words when different vowels are inserted. Traditionally, a reader identified a word by its context, but as fewer and fewer Jews were conversant in Hebrew, reading ancient texts became ever more difficult. There was a great

need to develop a system of indicating vowel sounds.

Over the years, three different groups of Masoretes developed systems of vocalization, but in the end the system developed by the ben Asher family won out. In this system, symbols – generally arrangements of dots – are placed above, below, or between the consonants, and accent marks are added to indicate pauses, stops, and accented syllables.

Five or six generations of the ben Asher family worked on this system. The last of these men, Moses ben Asher and his son Aaron, did the final work in perfecting it. In about 925, Aaron ben Asher himself used his system of notation to copy the manuscript known as the *Aleppo Codex* (because it was kept for centuries by a Jewish congregation in Aleppo, Syria). The system he used is the standard one to this day.

Fragments from the tenth-century *Aleppo Codex* – the earliest copy of the Hebrew Bible to use the Masoretic vowel markings.

New Alphabets for the Bible

SCRIPTURE FOR PEOPLES WITH NO WRITTEN LANGUAGE

While Christians in the Roman Empire were still debating which writings to include in the New Testament, a number of newly Christianized peoples on the outskirts of the empire were more concerned with how to read the Bible at all, whatever books it contained. Although these people had languages of their own, they had no system for writing. Beginning in the fourth century, a handful of amazing men developed alphabets for these new Christians and used these alphabets to translate the Bible into their everyday languages.

The first to benefit were the Visigoths (West Goths), a warlike group of Germanic tribes. Soon after, an Armenian developed alphabets for translating the Bible into the languages of three eastern European nations. Finally, Slavic peoples were given a Bible in their own tongue by two Greeks.

Ulfilas, the Little Wolf

Ulfilas (or Wulfila), said to have been the son of a Gothic raider and a Christian captive, was born in about AD 311 and, though his name means "Little Wolf", he became a Christian bishop instead of a warrior. Ulfilas was raised as a Christian and in about 340 he was consecrated bishop by Eusebius, the patriarch of Constantinople. Eusebius was an Arian, a movement that was later condemned as heresy, as it insisted Jesus was less than equal with God the Father.

For several years Ulfilas preached Arian Christianity, but was so persecuted by unbelieving Goths that in 348 he brought his congregation across the Danube River into Roman territory, where they settled in Moesia in what is now Bulgaria.

There, Ulfilas created a 27-letter Gothic alphabet made up of Greek and Roman letters plus two new ones. Then, using that alphabet, he began translating the Bible into Gothic.

No one knows how much Ulfilas translated, but it was probably not the entire Bible. His original Bible was lost, and the oldest surviving Gothic Bibles are far from complete. These copies, however, are the oldest surviving documents of any Germanic language. They are also the only known record of the Gothic language, which is now extinct.

Page from a ninth-century Visigothic Bible.

*We rightly praise the Slavonic letters invented by Cyril in which praises to God are set forth...
for he who created the three principal languages, Hebrew, Greek and Latin, also made the others
for his praise and glory.*

POPE ADRIAN II

An Armenian Bible – and Two More

Armenia, a small region beyond the eastern border of the Roman Empire, had become the world's first Christian kingdom in AD 313, when the king became a Christian – and his subjects followed suit. But for nearly a century Armenian Christians had to make do with Bibles in Greek and Syrian, which only a few Armenians understood. Then, in about 404, Mesrop, an Armenian monk who had studied the classical languages, developed an alphabet of 36 letters, using as his model the 24-letter Greek alphabet. Over the next five years he and a team of fellow linguists used that alphabet to translate the Bible into Armenian.

But Mesrop's work was not finished yet. Two neighbouring nations had also become Christian – Georgia and Caucasian Albania (in what is now Azerbaijan). Surprisingly, it was Mesrop who created alphabets for both kingdoms.

During missionary travels into Georgia, Mesrop created a 38-letter alphabet for translating the Bible into Georgian. Though it is uncertain when the translation work started and who did it, the Bible drew on Mesrop's alphabet. In his sixties, Mesrop travelled to Caucasian Albania, where he created a third alphabet that was used to translate the Albanian Bible.

Mesrop died in 440, at about the age of 80. He left behind not only the three alphabets, the Armenian Bible, and rituals, but also a collection of Bible commentaries, translations of the writings of the church fathers, and hymns. The Armenian and Georgian Bibles are still in use, but the Albanian Bible disappeared – along with the Albanian church – during the Islamic invasions of the seventh century.

CYRIL AND METHODIUS

In AD 862 the prince of Moravia (now Slovakia) called for missionaries to work with new Christians in his land. German missionaries there insisted on conducting rituals and reading the Bible in Latin, which few Slavs understood. Cyril and Methodius, brothers and highly educated priests from Thessalonica, Greece, answered the call.

Cyril developed a Slavonic alphabet and began translating the Bible and church rituals so that the people were able to worship in their own language. However, the German missionaries insisted that because the sign on Jesus' cross was written in Hebrew, Greek, and Latin, these should be the only languages used in church. They even appealed to Pope Adrian II, but the pope sided with the brothers.

Cyril died when he was only 42, and his brother completed the Slavonic Bible. After Methodius's death 15 years later, a new pope, Stephen V, banned the use of Slavonic in church, forcing followers of the brothers to leave the country. They scattered throughout Eastern Europe, taking their Slavonic language, Bible, and liturgy into neighbouring regions, including what is now Bulgaria, Yugoslavia, Romania, and Russia.

When the pope banned the use of the Slavonic language in Moravian churches, many Slavonic-speaking Christians moved to neighbouring regions, taking their Slavonic Bibles with them.

A Bulgarian tenth-century fresco of St Cyril (left) and St Methodius (right), Greek priests who produced a Slavonic Bible.

Monks and the Bible

LIFE AS A MONASTIC SCRIBE

Early hermits – including those from the time of Jerome and Augustine – deliberately left society and went out into the desert or some other out-of-the-way place. There they led lives of prayer and fasting, seeking to devote themselves to God's word as revealed in the Bible. Although few of these men and women had access to Bibles and fewer still could read, they regularly recited Scripture from memory. Later, hermits grouped together and eventually moved out of the desert into monasteries, where the written word became ever more important, and monks became the guardians of Scripture.

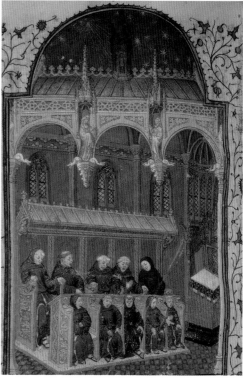

A fifteenth-century illumination from the psalter of King Henry VII of England, showing monks in their stalls.

St Benedict Praying with His Monks by Sodoma (sixteenth century).

Life of a Monk

A monk's life was governed by what was called a rule. The first rule, which was composed by the fourth-century Egyptian hermit Pachomius, became a model for all future ones. The most influential rule in the Western church was written in about 575 by Benedict of Nursia, abbot of the Italian monastery of Monte Cassino. Benedict's Rule, which stresses a life of work and prayer, is still followed today.

Under the Benedictine Rule – and its many variants – men or women lived in community, pledging obedience to the abbot, or head of the monastery, who was elected by the monks. The monks' waking hours were divided between work and prayer.

Many monasteries supported themselves by farming, so most of the monks spent their working hours in the fields. Others were assigned to take care of the daily running of the monastery. Whatever the monks did, they did for the glory of God, and they considered their work to be a form of prayer. However, they also spent hours a day engaged in formal prayer.

Formal prayer was of two types: private and community. Private prayer included *lectio divina* ("divine reading") in which the monk read a passage from the Bible or some other Christian text and meditated on its meaning in his own life.

Community prayer centred on the Divine Office, also called the Office of the Hours because its hymns, prayers, and sacred writings were sung, chanted, and read at specific hours each day. Each of the eight "hours" consisted of prayers and readings from Scripture, especially the Psalms. Generally the monks chanted all 150 psalms in the course of a week.

This illustrated Bible manuscript from the thirteenth century shows the rules that were used to guide the scribe while copying the text.

Preserving Scripture

Because books were needed for private reading and chanting the office, some monks were assigned to copying manuscripts. While the other monks laboured in the fields or the kitchen, these scribes painstakingly copied psalms, books of the Gospels, and sometimes entire Bibles. In addition, they copied lives of holy men and women, sermons, and biblical commentaries.

A Scribe Prepares

A scribe began his work by trimming his parchment to size, smoothing its surface with pumice, and rubbing it with chalk to remove any oil. He then added ruled lines to guide his hand in copying. Horizontal lines helped the monk keep his writing straight, vertical lines marked the margins, and other lines cordoned off space for artwork.

Next the scribe made pens by shaping the tips of hardened goose or swan feathers with a sharp (pen) knife. Because the pens did not hold their shape for long when in use they had to be sharpened constantly and replaced frequently. Reportedly a scribe used 60 to 100 pens a day.

The scribe also made black ink, generally by mixing charcoal or soot with plant gum or sap, and he made vermilion (red) ink from ground cinnabar or mercury sulphide. The red ink was used for chapter headings, titles, initials, and writing that was not part of the actual text. Because they were written in this red colour, extra-textual materials were called rubrics (from the Latin for "red"). The scribe poured the inks into pots or horns for use.

Copying a Manuscript

The scribe generally sat at a slanted desk, which helped him keep his pen perpendicular to the page. When he was ready to start copying, he placed a prepared parchment page on his desk beside the master text he was to copy. He then crouched over his work and carefully copied the master text. He held the pen in one hand and kept a knife in the other for sharpening the pen and scraping away errors.

Finally, the scribe proofread and corrected his work. He would recopy a page if it had serious flaws, but he might cross out repeated words, underline them with dots, or enclose them between the syllables of the Latin word *vacat* ("void"), which indicated that anything between "va" and "cat" should be ignored. He would squeeze omitted words in above the place where they belonged or write them in the margins. Some scribes also used the margins for observations about the text or personal notes. A few wrote in curses on anyone who might damage their hard work.

CHARLEMAGNE'S SCRIBE, ALCUIN

The Anglo-Saxon monk Alcuin was a brilliant scholar from York, who worked at the court of the emperor Charlemagne. In 796 Charlemagne made Alcuin abbot of the monastery of St Martin in Tours, France. There he made the scriptorium highly productive by utilizing a new lettering style.

Early manuscripts had been written in capital letters, called majuscules. These letters were unconnected to the letters that preceded and followed, forcing the scribe to lift his pen after writing each letter. This slowed the writing down and took up a lot of space. Earlier in the eighth century a new style of lettering called minuscule had come into use, and Alcuin is credited with perfecting it. In minuscule, the letters were connected and a scribe could write without stopping to lift his hand with each letter. Carolingian minuscule, as Alcuin's version is called, became the standard for European scribes.

Illuminating a Manuscript

CREATING A WORK OF ART

The earliest Christian manuscripts contained only words and so were somewhat off-putting to readers who were not dedicated scholars. To draw readers into their texts, monks began adding visual elements. In time, these elements became very elaborate and even incorporated gold to brighten the page. The light reflected by the gold lit up the page, or "illuminated" it. For this reason, manuscripts with gold (or silver) came to be known as illuminated. Today any lavishly decorated manuscript is labelled as such.

History of Illumination

The earliest book illustrations were on Egyptian papyrus scrolls from the second millennium BC, such as the Book of the Dead. No illustrated books survive after that time until the second century AD when Greek and Roman manuscripts included scenes depicted in the text.

Christians first illuminated their manuscripts in the fourth century. In time their illuminations became ever more diverse and elaborate, ranging from tiny decorative elements to full-page paintings. The margins were also sometimes filled with designs or scenes from the Bible.

In the sixth and seventh centuries, illumination declined as barbaric German tribes conquered much of Europe, decimating its culture. Unaffected by these invasions, however, Ireland and northern England continued to develop the art of illumination.

In the late eighth century, spurred on by the emperor Charlemagne, book illumination again flourished and continued to develop in the centuries that followed, taking on characteristics that reflected the cultures of the lands in which the manuscripts were created.

By the thirteenth century, illumination was mostly taken over by secular artists working for book dealers or individual patrons. After the invention of movable type in the fifteenth century, illuminated manuscripts gradually gave way to printed books with engraved illustrations.

Illuminated manuscript page showing Saul and the Battle of Mount Gilboa.

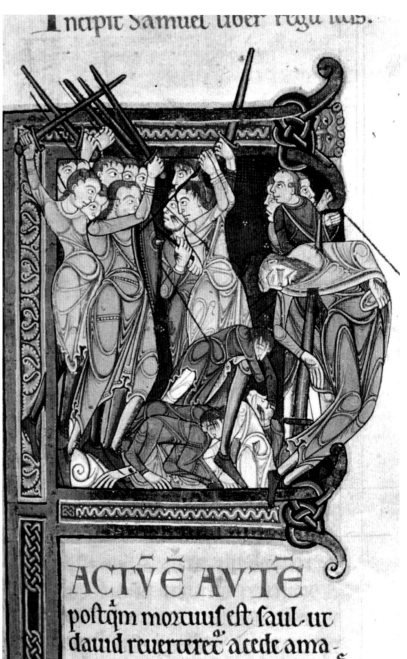

We who are a light to faithful souls everywhere, fall prey to painters knowing naught of letters, and are entrusted to goldsmiths to become, as though we were not sacred vessels of wisdom, repositories of gold leaf.

"COMPLAINT OF THE BOOKS" IN *PHILOBIBLION* BY RICHARD OF BURY, BISHOP OF DURHAM

Tools and Materials

Handmade pens and brushes, together with the all-important knife, were the illuminator's chief tools. He also needed a sharp metal or bone stylus – or a kind of graphite pencil – for sketching designs. In addition to black ink, he needed inks of various colours. Pigments for these colours came from a variety of sources, including cinnabar, oxidized copper, malachite, saffron, and lapis lazuli. The monk generally obtained these materials from an apothecary, pounded them into powder, and mixed with egg.

If the page was to include gold, the illuminator pounded a gold coin into extremely thin sheets of gold leaf. To hold the leaf in place on the page, the monk made a type of glue called glair from egg white. If a three-dimensional effect was desired, the artist built up the surface where the gold was to go with a plaster-like substance known as gesso. Finally, he used a tool made from a smooth rock or tooth to burnish the gold.

Illuminating a Page

The scribe who copied the text of a manuscript rarely illuminated it; generally, a separate artist or group of artists did so. If the manuscript contained geometric margin designs, a specialist in this type of painting might create those designs, leaving space for another artist to add animal or human figures. And yet another monk would apply gold leaf.

An artist started an illumination by making a rough design. Staying within the areas blocked off by the scribe, he would sketch out the design using a sharp stylus, and then go over the outline with thin ink to "crisp up" the design. Then he polished the areas inside the design to prepare them for decoration.

Gold leaf, if used, was applied at this point, as burnishing the gold might damage the colours if they were done earlier. First, the artist brushed a thin layer of glair on the area to be covered with gold, in order to make it adhere to the page. Then he cut a piece of foil to the size needed, carefully picked it up with a flat brush, or the moistened handle of a brush, and positioned it on the page. Once the gold was all in position, the artist burnished it with a special tool to bring out the lustre of the metal and seal it into place. Finally, the artist outlined the gold area with ink to smooth out any ragged edges.

The artist then added the colours one at a time and layer by layer to create various tones and shadings. Finally, he highlighted the design with white ink.

Above: This initial letter "B" incorporates an illustration of Jesus casting out demons (top) and the harrowing of hell (bottom). From the twelfth-century English Winchester Bible.

JEWISH ILLUMINATION

Jewish illumination had a late start because Mosaic law forbade the decoration of the Pentateuch. However, after a time, illuminations were used for the later books of the Bible, and by the thirteenth century, illuminated Jewish manuscripts were plentiful.

Styles of illumination varied with the locale, but most shared some common elements. The earliest illuminations focused on implements from the temple sanctuary, such as the menorah (seven-branched candelabra) or the ark of the covenant. Soon biblical commentaries began to illustrate legends, as in the Esther scrolls.

Nevertheless, Jews were reluctant to represent the human figure, because this was seen as violating the first commandment. In some manuscripts, human figures are shown, but they have the heads of birds or beasts. God is represented with a ray of light or an outstretched hand. There were also pages filled with geometric designs – known as carpet pages because they resembled the designs found in oriental carpets.

Illumination depicting a celebration inside a synagogue from a thirteenth- or fourteenth-century Haggadah (a book read during the Jewish Passover meal).

Bibles for Kings and Nobles

LAVISH ILLUSTRATED BIBLES

It was not only a gift fit for a king, it was designed for a king. The sumptuous *Bible moralisée*, or moralized Bible, was a book of biblical passages and commentary with 5,000 illuminations. Every page contained gold. The original book was produced between 1226 and 1240 and presented to Louis IX, the young king of France who was declared a saint after his death. It was later copied for other royal patrons. Those not privileged to receive a copy made do with lesser volumes, which they paid to have bound in precious metals and jewels.

Layout of Louis' Book

Every page of a *Bible moralisée* features four passages from the Bible, each with a brief commentary. Both biblical text and commentary are graced with illustrations that are set off in circular frameworks, or roundels. All this material is arranged in two columns. The first biblical passage appears in the upper left-hand corner of the page with an illustration to its right and a commentary just below. A second passage with commentary and illustration fills in the bottom of the first column. The right-hand column contains two more biblical passages with commentaries and illustrations in the same order as the first column.

The commentaries and illustrations in the *Bible moralisée* make it unique. In most medieval Bible books, Old Testament passages are used to foreshadow New Testament texts, showing how the New Testament fulfils the Old. The commentaries in the *Bible moralisée*, on the other hand, ignore New Testament parallels and focus on contemporary times, pointing out how biblical characters or situations show how medieval men and women fulfil or neglect their Christian duties.

A Humbler Picture Book

The *Bible moralisée* was not the only picture-book Bible. A much simpler book that used Bible illustrations to teach Christian morals was *The Mirror of Human Salvation*. It was probably created by Ludolph of Saxony in the early fourteenth century. Each of the book's more than 40 chapters illustrates a single New Testament scene that is accompanied by three scenes that predict or lead up to it.

Unlike other illustrated Bible books, which counterpose New Testament scenes with Old Testament scenes (or in the case of the *Bible moralisée* with contemporary scenes), *The Mirror of Human Salvation* also uses scenes from history and legend. For example, the death of Codrus, the last king of Athens, who deliberately brought about his own death in order to save his people from defeat, is seen as anticipating Jesus dying on a cross for the sins of all. The overall point of *The Mirror of Human Salvation* is that all history manifests God's plan for humanity.

Luxury Bible Covers

Medieval Bibles did not usually come bound and covered. People paid extra for that. Monks, and later artisans, began the process of binding by stacking folded sheets of the Bible in order. Then they stitched these "gatherings" with cord. Ends of the leftover cord were tied to what were often oak boards that provided the book's protective cover.

The bookbinders then decorated the plain wood covers with elaborate carvings or covered them in fine leather etched with intriguing patterns, floral motifs, or some other artwork. Some covers were inset with ivory plaques carved with Bible scenes. Others were carefully plated with thin layers of gold, silver, or brass with delicate artwork stamped or tooled into it. Still others were studded with jewels.

Artistry was limited only by the budget of the book owner and the skill of the artisan. For many of the wealthy, cost was no factor – they wanted nothing less than the best possible cover to encase the words of God.

This Italian Gothic Bible cover was probably commissioned by a wealthy Christian and donated to a church or monastery for use during services.

Dear Son, have a tender pitiful heart for the poor, and for all those whom you believe to be in misery of heart or body, and, according to your ability, comfort and aid them with some alms.

ADVICE OF KING LOUIS IX TO HIS SON

A gold-covered page from the *Bible moralisée*, which was presented to (Saint) Louis IX.

Medieval Worship

THE CYCLE OF SEASONS WITH BIBLICAL TEXTS

In the early days of the church, when Christianity was often outlawed, there was little communication between communities and almost no uniformity in worship services. Although the basics of reading from Scripture and celebrating the Eucharist were common, the prayers and the reading selections varied greatly. After Constantine gave official sanction to Christianity in 313, Christian worship moved into the open for the first time, taking place in large spaces. At that time more uniformity in worship was sought – and found.

This fourteenth-century French book illumination shows a congregation at worship.

The Liturgical Year

Christian worship came to be centred on a cycle of seasons that focused on events in the life of Jesus. The first of these seasons, Easter, went back to the early church. The first Christians observed the crucifixion and resurrection on the same day, but were soon remembering the crucifixion separately, on the Friday before Easter.

In the fourth century, Christian pilgrims visited the Holy Land to re-enact the events of the week leading up to the resurrection. In her diary, one pilgrim, Egeria, described a celebration of Holy Week in Jerusalem, and eventually Holy Week became part of the Christian calendar. The Easter season was eventually expanded to last 50 days, ending on Pentecost, which celebrates the descent of the Holy Spirit upon Jesus' disciples. In all these celebrations biblical passages appropriate to the events being recalled were read.

Because Easter was such a great feast, a period of fasting and preparation, called Lent, was observed. It eventually lasted 40 days, reflecting Jesus' 40 days in the desert. Readings were directed towards candidates for baptism.

By the fourth century Christmas was being celebrated on 25 December and preceded by Advent, a preparatory period of prayer and fasting. Advent readings focused on the coming of Jesus both as a child in Bethlehem and at the end of time.

The periods between these seasons are known as "ordinary time", because they do not include the four extraordinary seasons of Advent, Christmas, Lent, and Easter. Readings are chosen with an eye to including as much of the New Testament in the year's cycle as possible.

Books for Worship

The church's official prayers and rites make up what is known as the liturgy, or "work of the people", to distinguish them from private prayers. The liturgy includes the eucharistic service, prayers and rites for administering the other sacraments, and the Office of the Hours.

For use in church, biblical passages read during services were combined into lectionaries. Prayers said while offering the Eucharist and administering other sacraments were bound together in sacramentaries, and musical texts were put into antiphonaries. In the tenth century, all these materials were combined into books known as missals.

Lay people were left to worship privately on their own. However, in the thirteenth century, when books began to be produced outside the monasteries, some wealthy Christians commissioned their own prayer books – notably lavishly illustrated Books of the Hours. These books included quotations from the Gospels, sometimes prayers for the dead and the Hours of the Virgin – psalms and other texts devoted to Jesus' mother, Mary.

Christians without the means to buy books or the ability to read them relied on memorized prayers and their own thoughts. Some prayed the rosary, a series of 150 Hail Marys (the standard prayer to Jesus' mother), one for each of the 150 psalms. These prayers were divided into groups, or decades, of 10 Hail Marys, each preceded by the Lord's Prayer. During each decade the person praying meditated on a different "mystery" or event in the life of Jesus.

When we eat this Bread and drink this Cup, we proclaim your Death, O Lord, until you come again.

EUCHARISTIC PRAYER

● **SEE ALSO**
EARLY CHRISTIAN WORSHIP,
PP. 44–45

A page from the fifteenth-century *Book of Hours for Parisians* depicting the different monastic orders, shows the monks at service.

PILGRIMAGES TO THE HOLY LAND

For many Christians, reading the stories about Jesus was not enough. They wanted to walk where he walked, to put themselves on the very stage where all the Bible scenes were played out. Doing so, they believed, would strengthen their faith by helping bring the stories to life.

Christians probably began visiting sacred sites in the first century, but these visits were rare because of the intermittent persecutions of the Christians. Pilgrimages became popular, however, after the emperor Constantine legalized Christianity in 313. In fact, the emperor's own mother, Helena, made a pilgrimage to Jerusalem in 326. It is said that Helena found the cross on which Jesus died and had the Church of the Holy Sepulchre built there.

Typically, pilgrims visited places named in the Bible, tombs of prophets, and monuments to saints. They often went to Mount Sinai, retraced the exodus to the Promised Land, then visited Bible sites in what is now Israel – especially places where Jesus had walked.

Some early pilgrims kept diaries. Among them was a woman named Egeria, who from about 380 to 384 visited 63 Old Testament and 33 New Testament sites. Of her visit to Mount Sinai she wrote:

> *These mountains are ascended with infinite toil, for you cannot go up gently by a spiral track, as we say snail-shell wise, but you climb straight up the whole way, as if up a wall, and you must come straight down each mountain until you reach the very foot of the middle one, which is specially called Sinai… the holy mountain of God, where the law was given.*

Order of Worship

• •

Each eucharistic celebration began with preparatory prayers and a procession of the clergy to the altar. A lector read two biblical excerpts: one selected from the Gospels preceded by a related passage from elsewhere in the Bible. Then the priest gave a sermon, telling the people how to apply the readings to their everyday lives. The eucharistic celebration itself followed, and then the priest blessed the people and sent them home.

The interior of the Church of the Holy Sepulchre, Jerusalem.

Scholars Look at the Bible

SCHOLASTICISM AND HUMANISM EMERGE

The church led the way in education during the Middle Ages, and in the early twelfth century established the first universities – in Bologna, Paris, and Oxford. Since these schools were run by monks, it is not surprising that theology was the principal subject studied, but in time students also took classes in logic, public speaking, law, medicine, and theology – though theology was presented as the "Queen of the Sciences". Eventually, out of the expanded universities, there emerged two new movements: scholasticism, which searched for knowledge outside the Bible, and humanism, which used human logic and secular learning to re-evaluate and reform Christianity.

Scholastics Discover Aristotle

Under scholasticism, students were encouraged to seek knowledge and truth by venturing beyond the Bible and Christian faith. Faith and Scripture, while important, were not the only sources of wisdom. Scholars should also use their God-given powers of reason.

The opportunity to do so came with the rediscovery of the Greek philosopher Aristotle, a master of logic. Though Aristotle's ideas sometimes clashed with those of the Bible, the scholastics simply used ideas that seemed reasonable, and dropped any that clashed with their beliefs.

Aristotle's main gift to them was the practice of dialectics – the use of dialogue to separate truth from error. As an example, a teacher might raise a theological question, then hold a debate to find an answer based on reason. Using dialectics, scholastics were able to merge the sacred and the secular, while at the same time opening the door to a new world of questions.

The most important product of scholasticism was Thomas Aquinas's *Summa Theologica* ("Summary of Theology", 1267–73), a monumental attempt to provide a rational base for the mysteries in the Bible, showing that faith and reason are complementary ways of understanding the world.

Portrait of Thomas Aquinas (1225–74), painted by Fra Bartolommeo. Called the "Prince of Scholastics", Aquinas was an Italian theologian who taught at the University of Paris. He held that faith and reason were not enemies, but allies that could lead us to the truth.

Scholastic Aids to Biblical Study

As scholastics dug ever deeper into the Bible for answers to their questions, they found that they needed to read it in its original languages, not in a Latin translation. As a result, universities began to teach Hebrew and Greek.

Scholars also published biblical study aids, including atlases and manuals of plants and animals in Bible lands. In 1230, one scholar developed a concordance – an alphabetical list of words in the Bible and where they could be found. To make concordances work efficiently, however, indicators were needed to pinpoint particular passages in the Bible, which at the time was copied with no divisions.

From the early thirteenth century, various scholars had gradually introduced numbered chapters and then verse numbers to the Bible. Finally, in 1551, a scholar named Robert Estienne (Stephanus in Latin) published an entire Bible with chapter and verse numbers that are still used today.

> *I put up with this church, in the hope that one day it will become better, just as it is constrained to put up with me in the hope that I will become better.*
>
> DESIDERIUS ERASMUS

The "Prince of Humanists", Desiderius Erasmus (c.1466–1536).

Humanists Revise the New Testament

The first on record to correct mistakes in the Vulgate was Lorenzo Valla, a scholar from Italy. In 1455 he wrote *Annotations on the New Testament*, a work that angered conservatives but inspired a Dutch scholar named Desiderius Erasmus, who was later to be known as the "Prince of Humanism".

In 1504 Erasmus reprinted Valla's work and began writing a barrage of his own works that aimed at correcting abuses within the church. Erasmus wanted reform, not revolution, yet he was not beyond belittling a pope to get it. In one satire, he told of Pope Julius II being locked out of heaven by Peter, the first pope.

Erasmus's most influential work was a 1516 Greek edition of the New Testament, which he created by drawing from newly discovered Greek manuscripts – and adding a version of the Latin Vulgate translation.

Some of Erasmus's corrections to the Latin Bible raised questions about church rituals. In Mark 1:15, the Vulgate quotes Jesus as saying, "Do penance, and believe the gospel." But Erasmus quoted Jesus as saying, "Repent [be sorry] and believe the gospel." From this, Erasmus deducted that Christians did not need to confess their sins and "do penance" to make amends to God for their sins.

Church traditionalists were not impressed. Nor were they comforted by the humanist claim that a more accurate version of the Bible would produce better Christians.

Although Erasmus never wanted a theological revolution – and he later resisted the radical changes Martin Luther demanded – the Dutchman had set the stage. To quote a popular saying of the time: "Erasmus laid the egg and Luther hatched it."

Humanists Seek Reforms

As universities turned more and more to secular studies, a movement known as humanism emerged. Christian humanist scholars sought to apply insights they discovered in their secular studies to correct distortions preached and practised by many in the church.

In fact, the church had never been more corrupt. In the eyes of many the church had become a hostile institution committed to its own wealth and prestige at all costs. One of the low points came in 1492, when Roderigo Borgia, who had fathered 10 illegitimate children, was elected pope (Alexander VI) and cultivated a reputation for opulence, corruption, and murder. Nor was his successor any better. Pope Julius II dressed his troops in silver armour and financed his wars and massive building projects by selling both church offices and letters of indulgence that promised to reduce a person's time in purgatory.

Humanist scholars contended that centuries of misunderstanding about the Bible had led to distorted teachings, useless rituals, and scandalous behaviour. To correct such errors, they turned for guidance to the original Hebrew and Greek manuscripts of Scripture instead of to the church's traditional Latin Vulgate.

Pages from a 1522 edition of Erasmus's *De Ratione de Conscribendi Epistolas*. The markings are those of the censor of the Inquisition, 1747.

Wycliffe and His Bible

REBELLING AGAINST THE CHURCH

John Wycliffe, the Oxford scholar behind the first English Bible, instigated so much trouble in the church that, 43 years after he died, church leaders ordered his bones to be dug up, burnt to ashes, and thrown into a river.

This unlikely end sprang from an unlikely start. Wycliffe was born in about 1330 on a sheep farm, deep in the hinterlands of England. Had he stayed there, content with a simple education, the world might never have heard of him. But when he was about 16, he left home to study at Oxford, England's first and most prestigious university. He then remained at Oxford to teach, earning his reputation as the school's most brilliant theologian.

John Wycliffe.

Criticizing the Church

As Wycliffe studied the Bible, he came to believe that many church leaders were not practising what the Bible preached. So he spoke his mind. With his lectures, sermons, and writings, Wycliffe launched a vigorous campaign against the church, paving the way for the Reformation a century later.

When the church demanded financial support from England, which was currently experiencing its own financial difficulties, Wycliffe advised Parliament not to comply. He argued that Christ had called his disciples to poverty and the church was already too wealthy.

Wycliffe even criticized the pope. When Urban and Clement were each claiming to be pope and Urban called for war, Wycliffe replied, "How dare he make the token of Christ on the cross (which is the token of peace, mercy and charity) a banner to lead us to slay Christian men, for the love of two false priests." The pope, Wycliffe said, was not the voice of God on earth. The Bible was. He said the pope may not even be among those chosen for heaven.

The First English Bible

Driven by his lack of confidence in the authority of the church, as well as his respect for Scripture, Wycliffe started pushing for an English translation of the Bible, for only the well-educated clergy could read the Latin one. "The laity ought to understand the faith," Wycliffe said, "and, as doctrines of our faith are in the scriptures, believers should have the scriptures in a language they fully understand." Wycliffe commissioned a group of his followers – later given the derogatory name of Lollards ("mutterers") – to become travelling ministers who read the Bible and presented its teachings to people throughout the land.

Wycliffe may not have translated much or any of the Bible that bears his name. But at the very least he was the motivational force behind the project. Working from the Latin Vulgate, Wycliffe's followers produced two English translations. The first was a small pocket edition completed in about 1382. A surviving copy says that Nicholas of Hereford, one of Wycliffe's associates, translated the Old Testament. The New Testament translator is not named, but has traditionally been assumed to be Wycliffe. Many scholars, however, question Wycliffe's authorship because the language is much more stilted than that of the Bible quotations Wycliffe used in his sermons.

The 1382 Bible was hard to read because it was a literal translation of the Latin. A more reader-friendly version came out about a decade later – after Wycliffe's death – translated by his friend and secretary, John Purvey.

● **SEE ALSO**
TYNDALE, PP. 86–87
ENGLISH BIBLES FROM EXILE, PP. 90–91
KING JAMES VERSION, PP. 92–93

Englishmen learn Christ's law best in English. Moses heard God's law in his own tongue, so did Christ's apostles.

JOHN WYCLIFFE

READINGS FROM WYCLIFFE'S BIBLE

England at that time had three main dialects. Wycliffe and his followers chose to translate the Latin Bible into the Midland English dialect that was popular in the region around London. The Bible helped unite the English language. Here are excerpts from two familiar passages in Wycliffe's Bible compared with the same passages in the King James Version, translated more than two centuries later:

Forsothe God so louede the world, that he gaf his oon bigetun sone, that ech man that bileueth in to him perische not, but haue euerlastynge lyf.

For God so loved the world, that he gave his only begotten Son, that whosoever believeth in him should not perish, but have everlasting life.
John 3:16

If I speke with tungis of men and aungels, sothli I haue not charite, I am maad as bras sownnynge, or a symbal tynkynge.

Though I speak with the tongues of men and of angels, and have not charity, I am become as sounding brass, or a tinkling cymbal.
1 Corinthians 13:1

Page from the first English Bible, the translation of which was instigated by John Wycliffe in the late fourteenth century.

Opposition to the Wycliffe Bible

Church leaders bitterly opposed the English Bible. Henry Knighton, a contemporary writer, summed up the church's position:

Christ gave his gospel to the clergy and the learned doctors of the Church so that they might give it to the laity… Wycliffe, by thus translating the Bible, made it the property of the masses and common to all and more open to the laity, and even to women who were able to read… And so the pearl of the gospel is thrown before swine… The jewel of the clergy has been turned into the sport of the laity.

One pope issued five bulls (official letters) ordering Wycliffe's arrest. Two popes summoned him to Rome, and church leaders in England tried him three times. But his friends protected him and he was never in his lifetime convicted as a heretic.

The church regretted this and, in 1428, ordered his body to be unearthed. British historian Thomas Fuller, writing some 200 years later, describes what followed:

They burnt his bones to ashes and cast them into the Swift, a neighbouring brook running hard by. Thus the brook hath conveyed his ashes into Avon; Avon into Severn; Severn into the narrow seas; and they into the main ocean. And thus the ashes of Wycliffe are the emblem of his doctrine which now is dispersed the world over.

Bible Heroes and Heretics

SEEKING A LIFE OF POVERTY

In the Gospel of Matthew Jesus tells a rich young man: "If you wish to be perfect, go, sell your possessions, and give the money to the poor, and you will have treasure in heaven; then come, follow me" (Matthew 19:21). Between the twelfth and fifteenth centuries, when many corrupt church leaders lived in unconscionable luxury, a number of pious men – and their followers – took this passage to heart and sought to lead lives of poverty. Some criticized church leaders for failing to live in accordance with the Gospels, but others simply taught gospel values by example.

Arnold of Brescia Fights Greed

In the 1130s Arnold of Brescia, an Italian abbot, was so offended by the greed of some church leaders that he urged them to give away their wealth, live together in poverty, and share their few possessions, as described in the Acts of the Apostles.

However, Arnold was not content to seek change peacefully. He defiantly gave his support to the Roman senate in its rejection of the temporal power of the popes. He was eventually hanged and burnt and his ashes were thrown into the River Tiber.

Peter Waldo, founder of the Waldensians, in a nineteenth-century engraving.

Peter Waldo and the Waldensians

In about 1170 Peter Waldo (or Valdes), a rich merchant from Lyons, France, was converted when he heard the story of St Alexis, a fifth-century Roman patrician who had given all his wealth to the poor and lived the life of a beggar, hoping for true happiness in the next life.

Unable to read Latin, Waldo had biblical passages translated into French and set out on a life of begging, performing works of charity, and preaching that all Christians should imitate Christ by living in poverty.

Waldo soon attracted followers and sent them out two by two to teach the Scriptures. In 1179 the archbishop of Lyons ordered Waldo to stop preaching, but he refused. Two years later he appealed to Pope Alexander III, who approved of the lifestyle of the Waldensians (followers of Waldo) but not of their Bible translating and lay preaching.

Lay Waldensians continued to preach and in 1184 the Council of Verona condemned them as "pertinacious and schismatic". But this failed to stop them. Even after Waldo's death (between 1205 and 1218) his followers continued in their work. During the Reformation they formed their own church, which still survives.

Jan Hus

Jan Hus, a peasant from Bohemia who became a priest and scholar, was noted for his preaching in Czech. Drawing from the writings of John Wycliffe he held that Scripture, not the church hierarchy, should be the supreme authority for Christians. He also echoed Wycliffe in attacking the right of the church to own property rather than live according to gospel values.

Jan Hus is pictured here being burned at the stake.

At first Hus was supported by the archbishop of Prague, but later his sermons against the immorality of the clergy provoked hostility. In 1407 Hus was forbidden to preach, but he had the protection of the emperor, who made him rector of the university in Prague, which was heavily pro-Wycliffe. In 1410 Pope Alexander V ordered the destruction of Wycliffe's books and tried to keep Hus from preaching.

Hus attended the Council of Constance in 1415, where, despite the reassurance of a safe conduct from the emperor, he was put on trial, convicted of heresy, and burned at the stake. His martyrdom made him a great hero in Bohemia, and his followers – the Hussites – fought later religious factions in Bohemia.

The Humiliati

Still others who sought lives of poverty were the Humiliati, men and women who banded together to live lives of prayer, manual labour, and caring for the sick and poor. The Humiliati, who came mainly from Lombardy in northern Italy, also felt the need to preach, antagonizing church authorities, who insisted that only clergymen should preach. Because the Humiliati persisted, they were condemned at the Council of Verona in 1184.

The Humiliati, however, were less defiant than Arnold and Waldo had been, and in 1201 Pope Innocent III accepted them back into the church and even gave them permission to preach, provided they avoided theological matters and simply urged Christians to lead good lives. Unlike the Waldensians, the Humiliati bent to church authorities and were allowed to survive.

Francis, a Living Gospel

Where others had failed to live in poverty and reform the church, Francis of Assisi succeeded – by the power of his example and with the church's sanction.

The son of a wealthy Italian cloth merchant, young Francis pursued the riotous life of a knight in shining armour. In 1202, however, he was captured and kept in prison for a year. Later, while praying in a chapel, a voice from the crucifix said: "Repair my house." Francis sold some of his father's cloth to finance repairs to the chapel. When his father scolded him, Francis stripped naked in the public square,

Pope Innocent III Approves the Franciscan Rule by Giotto di Bondone.

disowned his earthly father in favour of his heavenly Father, and went on to live a life of dire poverty.

Francis did all he could to emulate Jesus. He rid himself of personal possessions, wore only a coarse habit, and begged on the streets. For his many followers, whom he called Friars Minor, he wrote a rule based on the Gospels and won approval for it from Pope Innocent III. He also wrote at least parts of the initial rules for the Poor Clares, an order of women headed by Clare of Assisi, and a Third Order for lay men and women who followed his ideals while living with their families.

Francis so closely imitated Jesus that he was known as "the other Christ". Unable to ignore him, even the corrupt clergy were forced to institute reforms. And so Francis did indeed repair Christ's house, as earlier instructed. He died on 3 October 1226.

The Bible Goes to Press

THE GUTENBERG BIBLE AND BEYOND

A German metalworker probably takes as much responsibility as Martin Luther for the religious revolution that split the Western Church into Catholic and Protestant. His name was Johann Gutenberg, and he was a pioneer in printing.

Although John Wycliffe, Jan Hus, and others had stirred up sparks of reform, the fire had not spread. Luther's reform message, however, would spread like a wild fire. The reason? Luther used Gutenberg's new printing press to print and spread his message to hundreds of thousands of people and to publish the Bible itself in his people's own language.

Setting up Shop

Gutenberg grew up in Mainz, Germany, but in the 1430s he moved to Strasbourg, France, where he somehow developed his printing press. Apparently a carpenter loaned Gutenberg money to build a screw-driven wooden press, and a goldsmith provided printing materials for "new art". Gutenberg then probably cut the metal letters he would later use for printing. In the late 1440s Gutenberg returned to Mainz and set up a printing shop, where he produced a poem about Judgment Day, calendars for 1448, and, ironically, church indulgences.

The First Printed Bible

In about 1450 Gutenberg sought financial backing to print a Latin Vulgate Bible. Over the next several years Johann Fust, a wealthy banker, loaned him 1,600 guilders. In 1454 Gutenberg showed samples of his forthcoming Bible at a trade fair, and found buyers for all 180 copies he planned to print. In late 1455, though, as the Bible project was wrapping up, the banker and the printer quarrelled. Fust wanted his money back with interest – a total of about 2,020 guilders. The case went to court, and Gutenberg was forced to give the banker both his equipment and his Bible. Fust and Gutenberg's assistant, Peter Schöffer, finished printing the Bible.

Forty-eight copies of the two-volume Bible still exist. Each of the Bible's 1,282 pages has 2 columns of, usually, 42 lines (which is why it is called the "42-Line Bible"). To make the text look handwritten, Gutenberg had fashioned several designs for each letter, ending up with 270 letters plus 125 symbols and abbreviations.

Although Gutenberg never signed his work, many believed he opened another shop and printed a 36-line Bible in 1458.

Other Early Printed Bibles

The art of printing spread rapidly, and by 1500 there were printing shops in most European cities, and more than 90 editions of the Latin Vulgate had been printed. Bibles in local languages were also printed, including a German Bible in Strasbourg in 1466 and a Czech translation in 1475.

The earliest printed books were generally not illustrated or decorated, although the printer usually left space for artwork to be added after printing. Still, some colour work was done on the press. Notably, in 1457 Johann Fust and Peter Schöffer, who had completed the printing of the Gutenberg Bible, produced a psalter in which certain letters were printed in red, and some background designs in blue. In order to produce the three colours the printers had to put the pages through the press three times. In about 1475 printers began inserting woodcuts into their pages, and woodcuts were used extensively in printed books for centuries to come.

A hand-painted page from the Gutenberg Bible.

MAKING PAPER

The Chinese invented paper in the second century, but kept the process of making it a secret for centuries, which assured them a monopoly. To make the paper, they put insoluble fibres – such as bark, leaves, or rags – into a vat of water and soaked and hammered them until the fibres broke down and became suspended in the solution. They then dipped a page-sized mould with a fine mesh bottom into the vat and drained out the water. This left a thin sheet of material that was put into a press to squeeze out more water, then hung out to dry.

The first European papermaking mill was set up in Spain in about 1150. The quality of early European paper was poor, but by the time printing had begun, papermakers had perfected their art and paper was widely used for printed books from then on.

Left: Reconstruction of Gutenberg's printing press.

BLOCKBOOKS

Shortly before books were first printed from movable type, they were printed from immovable type that was carved into blocks of wood. To create a blockbook page, text and pictures were carved into the wood, covered with ink, then pressed against paper.

Shown here is a page from the *Biblia Pauperum* ("Bible for the Poor" – or for poor readers). This fifteenth-century German blockbook is a highly illustrated volume of related Bible stories. The central illustrations depict Samson escaping death by tearing up the gates of Gaza and carrying them to Hebron (left); Jonah being spat out of the mouth of the great fish (right); and Jesus rising from the tomb (centre). Blockbooks continued to be made even after the time of Gutenberg, with its heyday running from about 1550 until 1575.

The Printer's Art

Gutenberg made his so-called movable type by hand-cutting individual letters onto the tip of hard metal rods and pressing each letter into soft metal. He then filled the punched-out area with a strong, molten alloy. When the alloy hardened and was removed, it formed the mirror view of a letter and was stored in an organizer box.

To build a page, a printer pulled letters from the box, arranged them in a metal frame, and locked the frame to hold the letters in place. He then dabbed thick ink on the letters and clamped a sheet of paper into a holder above the text plate. Finally, he pushed a bar attached to huge vertical screws – like smaller screws that push up car jacks today – to lower a metal plate, pressing the inked type and paper together. The printed sheets were then hung to dry.

Luther and His Bible

THE REFORMATION HITS ITS PEAK

German Bible scholar Martin Luther, a one-time monk, is most famous for starting the Reformation, a movement that ended up splitting the Western Church in two: Catholic and Protestant. But Luther also translated the Bible into everyday German, which helped unify the nation with its diversity of dialects. Surprisingly, Luther took only 11 weeks to finish the first draft of his New Testament – part of a Bible translation so plainspoken that revised copies of it are still popular among Germans today.

Letter of indulgence, with papal seals hanging from the bottom.

A portrait of Martin Luther (1483–1546) by Lucas Cranach the Elder.

I Will Become a Monk!

Luther was the son of a copper miner who financed his son's education. After earning a master's degree, Luther began to study law. Then, one day, he was caught on the road in a dangerous thunderstorm and cried out to the patron saint of miners, "Help me, St Anne! I will become a monk!" Soon after, Luther entered an Augustinian monastery, and after a time was assigned to teach Scripture at the University of Wittenberg.

Luther became captivated by the Bible's teaching that Christians are saved not by obeying church rules, confessing sins to a priest, and doing penance. They are saved simply by trusting God. One verse summed it up for him: "The one who is righteous will live by faith" (Romans 1:17). Luther's studies convinced him that he did not need to earn God's salvation. He simply needed to accept it as a gift.

Heaven for Sale

Luther's new insight came at a time when the church was dealing badly with a financial crisis. To raise money, Pope Leo X had created and sold more than 2,000 church jobs. He also approved the sale of indulgences – spiritual fast-pass tickets into heaven. The argument supporting the sale of indulgences was that the church had a vast spiritual treasury built up by the good works of Jesus, the apostles, and the saints. The pope could draw on these resources to release people from penance in the after-life realm of purgatory and send them to heaven.

Generally travelling salesmen sold the indulgences and sent most of the proceeds to the pope. The man who hawked indulgences in

● SEE ALSO
THE BIBLE GOES TO PRESS,
PP. 82–83

Germany was a hard-sell monk named Johann Tetzel, who would announce, "Listen to the voice of your dear dead relatives and friends beseeching you and saying, 'Pity us, pity us. We are in dire torment from which you can redeem us for a pittance.'" Tetzel often ended his pitch with a jingle: "As soon as the coin in the coffer rings, the soul from purgatory springs."

Luther Protests

In response, Luther wrote his famous Ninety-Five Theses – statements against the sale of indulgences, against abuses within the church, and against teachings that salvation requires confession to a priest as well as penance. He nailed these to the door of All Saints' Church in Wittenberg on 31 October 1517, hoping to spark a debate that would ignite a cleansing blaze of reform. Instead, he was excommunicated.

Three and a half years after posting his theses, Luther was put on trial by the Holy Roman Emperor Charles V at the Diet of Worms (which means the meeting in the German city of Worms). When asked to recant, Luther said, "Unless I can be instructed and convinced with the evidence from the holy scripture or with open, clear and distinct grounds of reasoning… then I cannot recant."

The emperor ruled: "A single friar who goes counter to all Christianity for a thousand years must be wrong." To keep Luther safe, a local prince kidnapped him and put him in protective custody in a castle.

A Bible for the German People

During the 10 months he spent in the castle, Luther translated the New Testament into German. Working from the Greek New Testament by the Dutch scholar Erasmus, Luther completed the first draft in a mere 11 weeks.

Luther avoided making a rigid translation by not following the Greek word patterns too closely. Rather, he wanted Scripture to read the way Germans spoke. "To translate properly", Luther explained later, "is to render the spirit of a foreign language into our own idiom. I try to speak as men do in the marketplace. In rendering Moses, I make him so German that no one would suspect he was a Jew."

Luther submitted his translation for review by a committee of gifted scholars, and his New Testament – *Das Neue Testament Deutzsch*

Luther defends his beliefs before Holy Roman Emperor Charles V in Anton von Wrener's painting *Luther at the Diet of Worms*.

– was published in September 1522 and priced at about a week's salary for a typical worker. A printer's masterpiece, with beautiful type and woodcut illustrations, it sold more than 100,000 copies in Luther's lifetime.

The Old Testament came next, but it took 12 years because Luther worked from a variety of Hebrew texts, and he was not as familiar with Hebrew as he was with Greek. In addition, he also took pains to understand topics that were unfamiliar to him. When writing about sacrificial rituals, he had the town butcher cut up a sheep so he could study its organs.

Luther ultimately wrote many scholarly works, but he considered his translation of the Bible to be his greatest contribution to the world: "I'd like all my books to be destroyed so that only the sacred writings in the Bible would be diligently read."

First page of the Letter to the Romans in Luther's German New Testament.

More Reformation-Era Bibles

VERNACULAR BIBLES IN SIXTEENTH-CENTURY EUROPE

Throughout the sixteenth century, the reforms instigated by Martin Luther spread throughout Europe, as did Bibles in the languages of the people. Catholic leaders continued to fight the publication of Bibles in modern languages. They argued that they may introduce errors or that readers who were not grounded in theology may misinterpret what they read. But they also worried that these Bibles might encourage the reforms being sought by the "Protestants". Indeed, many did incorporate material that promoted Protestant ideas.

The opening of Matthew's Gospel from Tyndale's English Bible.

William Tyndale is tied to a stake, strangled with a rope, and then burnt. Woodcut from 1563, published in John Foxe's *Acts and Monuments*.

Tyndale: Translator on the Run

Because of Catholic opposition in England (soon to be a Protestant nation), William Tyndale, a priest and linguist, was denied permission to translate the Bible into English. Not to be stopped, Tyndale moved to Hamburg, Germany, where he finished translating Erasmus's Greek New Testament into English in 1525. In Cologne, while the book was being printed, anti-Protestants raided the print shop. The printing was finished in Worms and 6,000 copies were smuggled into England, in barrels of flour and bolts of cloth.

Infuriated, church leaders in England burnt all the copies of Tyndale's translation they could acquire and sent agents to hunt down Tyndale and arrest him. Meanwhile Tyndale published corrected editions of his New Testament in 1534 and 1535, and worked on translating the Old Testament, which he never completed.

Tyndale was tried and executed in 1536 – not for publishing an English New Testament, but for holding Luther-like beliefs. Among other things, the introductions and notes in his translations advocated salvation through faith, not the church.

A year after Tyndale's execution, Bibles that drew heavily on his work circulated in England with the approval of King Henry VIII. Within five years, churches faced fines if they did not have Bibles in English available for all the people.

The Bible Speaks in Many Tongues

The success and wide availability of Luther's Bible led German Catholics to publish their own error-free Bibles in German. Ironically, these were mainly adaptations of Luther's work. The first, by Hieronymus Emser, simply brought Luther's translation more in line with the Latin Vulgate. The second, which became the standard German Catholic Bible, was a revision of Emser's work by Johann Dietenberger. It used Luther's Old Testament, a translation by Anabaptists (a radical Protestant group), and a Bible that had been published in Zürich in 1529.

Other Bibles that appeared in European languages during the sixteenth century include:

See Also
LUTHER AND HIS BIBLE, PP. 84–85
ENGLISH BIBLES FROM EXILE,
PP. 90–91

> *If God spares my life for a few years, I'll see to it that a boy pushing the plough knows more of the Bible than you do.*
>
> WILLIAM TYNDALE, SPEAKING TO THE CLERGY

Dutch: Spurred by the Reformation, a number of Dutch Bibles appeared. The one published by Jacob van Liesveldt in 1526 became so popular that, in 1548, the Catholics published their own Dutch Bible.

Icelandic: A New Testament, based on the Vulgate and Luther, was published in 1540, and a complete Bible in 1584.

Swedish: After achieving independence from Denmark in the early sixteenth century, Sweden published its own New Testament, based on Luther, the Vulgate, and Erasmus's Greek New Testament. The first official complete Bible followed in 1541.

Hungarian: A New Testament was translated from the Greek in 1541, but the occupation of the Turks and opposition of the Catholics resulted in a halt to printing Bibles in Hungarian. The first complete Hungarian Bible was not issued until 1590, when it became the Bible of the Protestant Church in Hungary.

Danish: Two years after the publication of Luther's New Testament, a Danish version was made at the request of exiled King Christian I. In 1550 a complete Bible was published on command of King Christian II. It was revised in 1589 and again in 1633.

Polish: A New Testament translation was made from the original Greek by the Lutheran scholar Jan Seklucjan in 1553. A complete Bible made at Brest from the original languages followed in 1563. A revision of the Brest Bible was made for the Unitarians, and yet another revision, the Danzig Bible of 1632, became the official Bible of all the Evangelical Churches in Poland.

Serbo-Croatian: A New Testament appeared in 1562–63. Because the Serbian and Croatian languages are identical, only a single translation was needed, but since they use different alphabets, they had to be published separately in Glagolitic and Cyrillic.

Slovene: A complete Bible was published in 1584 for the Slovene-speaking provinces of Austria.

French: Although basically a Catholic country, France issued a number of French Bibles that were influenced by the Reformation. The New Testament, which was probably the work of the reformer Jacques LeFèvre d'Étaples, was published in Paris in 1523. A French Old Testament appeared in Antwerp in 1528 and the two Testaments were published together as the Antwerp Bible in 1530. In 1535 a true Protestant version was prepared by Pierre Robert, known as Olivétan. It was frequently revised, notably by the reformer John Calvin in 1546 and in 1553 by the French printer–scholar Robert Estienne (Stephanus in Latin). In response, Catholics published a new version, known as the Louvain Bible, in 1550.

Italian: The first Protestant Bible in Italian was made by the Greek and Hebrew scholar Giovanni Diodati and published in Geneva in 1607, revised in 1641, and frequently reprinted.

Portuguese: Because of the Inquisition, publication of a Portuguese New Testament did not occur until 1681. The first complete Portuguese Bible did not appear until 1748–53.

Spanish: In Spain, the Inquisition forbade the publication of the Bible in the language of the people, so no Spanish Bibles were published until the eighteenth century.

A portrait of the Protestant reformer John Calvin. The theological father of Southern Baptists, Presbyterians, and other churches in the Reformed tradition, Calvin developed the first carefully reasoned, systematic, Bible-based theology for Protestants, which included his doctrine of predestination – the teaching that God decides who will and will not be saved, and humans can do nothing about it. Calvin was also a noted biblical commentator.

A Catholic Response

THE COUNCIL OF TRENT

Faced with the spread of Protestantism, the Catholic Church was forced to look into itself, acknowledge its faults, and initiate reforms. Many Catholics called for a general church council to deal with these issues, but when Emperor Charles V asked Pope Clement VII to call one, he refused. The pope was afraid that such a council might issue decrees that would reduce the pope's power – and income. Entertaining the same fears, Clement's successor, Paul III, attempted to make reforms on his own, but when pressured by Charles V, he relented. After a few false starts, the council opened at Trent, in northern Italy, in December 1545. It continued – with two long interruptions – until December 1563.

Portrait of Pope Paul III with his nephews Ottavio and Alessandro Farnese by Titian (1468–1549).

A depiction of the Council of Trent.

Responses to Protestants

During its 25 sessions the Council of Trent reaffirmed many of the Catholic Church's old beliefs and practices and condemned various Protestant doctrines – notably, Martin Luther's doctrine of justification by faith alone.

The council also reaffirmed that Christ had instituted seven sacraments – baptism, confirmation, the Eucharist, penance (reconciliation), extreme unction (anointing of the sick), holy orders, and matrimony. In contrast, Protestants accepted only baptism and the Eucharist. In addition, contrary to the claim of some Protestants, the presence of Jesus in the Eucharist was said to be real and not symbolic. Other council decrees reaffirmed the existence of purgatory, veneration of relics and images, and invocation of the saints in prayer. Although Luther had been violently opposed to indulgences, the council declared them valid. However, moderation was urged and the taking of fees for granting indulgences was forbidden.

Pronouncements on Scripture

Decrees on Scripture came in the fourth session, held in 1546. Countering Luther's doctrine that the source of Christian truth was to be found in Scripture alone, the council upheld the validity of Christian tradition, which was believed to have been passed down from the apostles.

The same decree enumerated the books of the Bible. They included the books Protestants regard as the Apocrypha – books that appear in the Septuagint (the ancient Greek translation of the Hebrew Scriptures) but not in the standard Hebrew Bible. In the fourth century, Jerome in his Vulgate had been the first to label these books Apocrypha, noting that they should not be considered part of the Old Testament canon. However, over the centuries Jerome's reservations had been forgotten, and these books had come into general use within the church. Trent declared

Let no one dare to interpret the scripture in a way contrary to the unanimous consensus of the Fathers, even though such interpretations not be intended for publication.

DECREE OF THE COUNCIL OF TRENT

them canonical, and they remain so today for Catholics. Protestants generally group the Apocrypha together and position them between the Old and New Testaments or in a kind of appendix. Although Protestants did not totally reject these works, they did not treat them as equal to the other books.

In another decree, the council declared the Catholic Church to be the only legitimate interpreter of Scripture "to restrain irresponsible minds" from distorting the meaning of God's word. It also named the Vulgate the authoritative text of the Bible because it had been "preserved by the Church for so many centuries". The Vulgate was to be used in all "public readings, disputations, sermons and expositions". However, the council did implicitly acknowledge that the Vulgate contained imperfections, for it demanded that it be printed "in the most correct version possible". After the council ended, scholars began work on a revised Vulgate, which was finally published under Pope Clement VIII in 1592. This Clementine Vulgate has remained the official Latin version of the Bible ever since.

Cardinal Francisco Ximénez de Cisneros (1436–1517), archbishop of Toledo.

POLYGLOT BIBLES

The renewed interest of Catholics in pinpointing the most accurate form of the Bible's texts led scholars to make more use of a fairly new type of study Bible – books that contained the biblical texts in the original language together with ancient translations. Such books are called polyglot Bibles because "poly" means many and "glot" means language.

The idea of publishing a polyglot Bible originated with Cardinal Francisco Ximénez de Cisneros, archbishop of Toledo, Spain. He may have derived the idea from the sixfold Bible (*Hexapla*) of the third-century scholar Origen. Although Origen had copied biblical texts into six columns (one column for each version), he included only Hebrew and Greek versions. Cardinal Ximénez added Latin and Aramaic.

The work on the first polyglot Bible was done between 1514 and 1517 by a team of scholars at a university in Alcalá de Henares, Spain. The Latin name for the city of Alcalá, Complutum, gave its name to the work. It is known as the *Complutensian Polyglot*.

The Old Testament is printed in three columns, containing texts of the standard Hebrew (Masoretic) version, the Greek Septuagint (the earliest Greek translation of the Old Testament), and the Latin Vulgate. For the first five books of the Bible (the Pentateuch) Aramaic targums (paraphrases), printed in Hebrew characters, appear at the bottom of each page along with Latin translations of the targums. The New Testament texts are printed in two columns, one for the original Greek and the other for the Latin. The six-volume Bible also contained a Hebrew grammar, and Hebrew and Aramaic vocabulary lists.

At Antwerp, between 1569 and 1572, the French printer Christopher Plantin published an elaborate polyglot Bible, which included a Syriac version of the New Testament – along with a Latin translation of the Syriac. (Syriac was an Aramaic dialect used in some Eastern churches.) Between 1629 and 1645, a 10-volume polyglot Bible was published in Paris, which added Arabic versions of the Bible and the Samaritan Pentateuch. Finally, the London Polyglot Bible, perhaps the finest of them all, appeared between 1654 and 1657. It contained texts in nine languages: Hebrew, Aramaic, Samaritan, Greek, Latin, Ethiopic, Syriac, Arabic, and Persian.

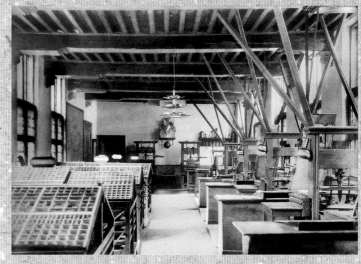

Christopher Plantin's printing works, shown here, are preserved in a museum in Antwerp, Belgium.

XIMÉNEZ DE CISNEROS

English Bibles from Exile

CATHOLIC AND PROTESTANT TRANSLATIONS

The sixteenth century was a period of religious upheaval in England. In 1534 King Henry VIII broke away from the Catholic Church when the pope refused to acknowledge his divorce from Catherine of Aragon and his remarriage to Anne Boleyn. For the remainder of his reign Henry adopted a form of high Protestantism, as did his son, Edward VI, who reigned from 1547 to 1553. Edward was succeeded by his half-sister, Mary I, who reinstated Catholicism as the state religion. When Mary died in 1558, she was succeeded by Elizabeth I, who had been declared illegitimate by the Catholic Church, which had never accepted Henry's marriage to her mother, Anne Boleyn. Elizabeth, predictably, reinstated Protestantism as the state religion. During all this time Protestants and Catholics fell into and out of favour, and at various times those out of favour produced their own English-language translations of the Bible – from exile.

Mary I, queen of England from 1553 to 1558, promoted Catholicism and persecuted Protestants. This portrait is by Master John (1544).

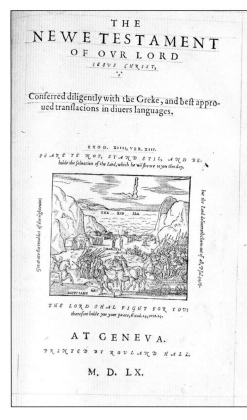

THE
NEWE TESTAMENT
OF OVR LORD
IESVS CHRIST,

Conferred diligently with the Greke, and beft appro-
ued tranflacions in diuers languages.

EXOD. XIIII, VER. XIII.
FEARE YE NOT, STAND STIL, AND BE-
holde the faluation of the Lord, which he wil fhewe to you this day.

THE RED SEA
ISRAELITES
EGYPTIANS

THE LORD SHAL FIGHT FOR YOV:
therefore holde you your peace, Exod.14, ver.14.

AT GENEVA.
PRINTED BY ROVLAND HALL.

M. D. LX.

Title page for the New Testament section of the 1560 Geneva Bible, the Bible of Shakespeare and Milton and long the favourite of the Puritans.

The Geneva Bible for Protestants

Queen Mary so fiercely attacked the Protestants of England that she came to be known as Bloody Mary. For their own safety, many Protestant scholars fled the country. Some settled in Geneva, Switzerland, where they gathered together under John Knox, the Scottish reformer, who was pastor of an English church there. Because Queen Mary had forbidden publication of English Bibles in her realm, the Protestant exiles prepared their own.

William Wittingham, who had been a Fellow at Oxford, did most of the translating. His English version of the New Testament was published in Geneva in 1557. When Mary died and the Protestant Elizabeth I came to the throne, many of the exiles returned home, but Wittingham remained in Geneva, where he published his Old Testament in 1560. The full Bible was published in England in 1576.

The Geneva Bible was compact and relatively inexpensive, and it contained features that made it easier to read – including clear type, verse numbers, vivid illustrations, maps, notes, and prefaces. It was also the best English translation to date. Consequently it was very popular and it remained so even after the publication of the King James Version. It was the Bible of the great writers of the seventeenth century – including Shakespeare, Bunyan, and Milton – and it was taken by the Puritans to the English colonies in America.

● SEE ALSO
KING JAMES VERSION, PP. 92–93

> ... *we presume not in hard places to modifie the speaches or phrases, but religiously keepe them word for word, and point for point, for feare of missing or restraining the sense of the holy Ghost to our phantasie.*
>
> PREFACE TO THE DOUAI–RHEIMS NEW TESTAMENT

Elizabeth I, queen of England from 1558 to 1603, promoted Protestantism and persecuted Catholics. This portrait is after Nicholas Hilliard (c.1575/80).

The Douai–Rheims Bible for Catholics

Just as Protestant scholars fled from England during Mary's reign, Catholic scholars fled from the reach of the staunchly Protestant Elizabeth. Some established an English college in Douai (then part of Flanders, but later ceded to France).

In 1578 they began work on an English translation of the Bible in order to counter what they saw as the corruptions of heretics. In 1582 the New Testament was published in Rheims, France, where the college had moved temporarily. The Old Testament was published back in Douai in 1609.

In a preface, the translators insist that they followed only the Latin Vulgate version approved by the church, although it is obvious that they also made use of the Greek and Hebrew texts and even the "heretical" translations they condemned, especially the Geneva Bible. They also tell us that they made their translation as literal as possible.

The Douai–Rheims Bible remained the official English translation for Catholics until well into the twentieth century. For the most part, the translation is excellent, though faithfulness to the text sometimes resulted in strange expressions. Some of these became part of the English language, including "advent", "character", "evangelize", and "victim". Others remain obscure, such as "potestates", "longanimity", and "correption". And Matthew's version of the Lord's Prayer reads in part, "give us this day our supersubstantial bread". In time, some of the odd expressions were replaced, but not "supersubstantial bread".

OTHER ENGLISH BIBLES

In addition to the Bibles translated from exile, other English Bibles that appeared during the reigns of Henry VIII and Elizabeth I included:

The Coverdale Bible	Matthew's Bible	The Great Bible	The Bishops' Bible
The Coverdale Bible was put together by Miles Coverdale, who had worked with William Tyndale on his Old Testament translations. However, not knowing enough Hebrew or Greek to translate from the original languages, Coverdale relied on the Latin Vulgate and on translations by Luther, Tyndale, and others. The influence of Coverdale's Bible, which appeared in 1535, was limited.	Matthew's Bible, which was printed in 1537, was more successful. It was edited by John Rogers, a friend of Tyndale's. Working under the name Thomas Matthew, Rogers did not translate the Bible anew, but used Tyndale's New Testament and as much of the Old Testament as Tyndale had completed. For the rest, he used Coverdale's translation. Henry VIII's chancellor, Thomas Cromwell, convinced the king to approve this Bible.	The Great Bible was published in 1539, in response to a request by Henry VIII for a large-sized Bible that could be placed in churches for the people to read. (Matthew's Bible was rejected for this purpose because many of its notes reflected a radical Protestantism that was not acceptable.) Consequently, Cromwell assigned Coverdale to revise Matthew's Bible and financed the project himself. The Great Bible, over 25 centimetres (14 inches) tall, is named for its size.	The Bishops' Bible was published in 1568 – after Elizabeth I had come to the throne and the Geneva Bible was being printed in England. Conservative churchmen, disapproving of the Puritan bent of the notes in the Geneva Bible, sought to prepare a more acceptable translation, based mainly on the Great Bible. The work was done by 16 scholars, mainly bishops. The translation was far inferior to the Geneva version, which remained the people's favourite.

King James Version

THE GREATEST OF ALL ENGLISH BIBLES

W hen James VI of Scotland became James I of England in 1603, he was greeted with a petition signed by 1,000 Puritans who wanted to purify the Church of England of leftover Catholic influences. King James agreed with the Puritans in only one main thing. There was a need for a new Bible – though the Puritans disliked the Bishops' Bible because it was not Protestant enough and James hated the Geneva Bible because its running commentary was too Protestant.

In 1604, at a meeting to evaluate the state of the church in England, James announced he would like an accurate translation of the Bible to replace the other English versions and to become the only version read in church. He wanted the work done by England's best Bible scholars and linguists. And he did not want any commentary added to the margins.

King James I of England in a portrait by Paul van Somer.

Getting Started

That same year the king submitted to Richard Bancroft, bishop of London, a list of men he had chosen for the project. The men were divided into 6 teams and given 15 rules to guide them, including:

- The new version was to follow the Bishops' Bible as much as possible.

- Translators were free to draw from many other versions in an attempt to find the best way of expressing the message contained in the original Bible languages.

- There would be no marginal notes except those needed to clarify Hebrew and Greek words or to point out related Bible passages. This was to allow the Bible to speak for itself, and to keep translators from inserting their own interpretations.

- Translators were to retain traditional church office terms instead of substituting terms that many Protestants preferred. For example, the translators were to use "priest" instead of "elder" and "church" instead of "congregation".

Each of the six teams translated different parts of the Bible and then submitted their work for review to a committee of 12 scholars, made up of two men from each translation team.

A New Bible

It took the teams about three years to finish their initial drafts, sometimes working individually and sometimes in conference. Another three years were spent in review and revision. The translators were meticulous and made no apologies for being more concerned about the quality of their work than the speed.

The result of their work was a black-letter edition measuring 41 by 27 centimetres (16×10.5 inches). It was published in London in 1611 and dedicated to King James, who had ordered the project. It has been known since as the King James Version, or sometimes the Authorized Version.

COMMON PHRASES FROM THE BIBLE

We still use phrases coined by the King James Version, including:

Skin of my teeth (Job 19:20)

You cannot take it with you (Ecclesiastes 5:15)

A leopard cannot change its spots (Jeremiah 13:23)

At wits' end (Psalm 107:27)

Blind leading the blind (Matthew 15:14)

● SEE ALSO
ENGLISH BIBLES FROM EXILE,
PP. 90–91

We did not disdain to revise that which we had done and to bring back to the anvil that which we had hammered.

TRANSLATORS OF THE KING JAMES VERSION OF THE BIBLE

THE CHANGING ENGLISH BIBLE

The King James Version, many say, was not so much a new translation as a revision of earlier English Bibles. To illustrate this, here is a comparison of how several English versions translated the first two verses of Psalm 23:

The Lord gouerneth me, and no thing schal faile to me;
in the place of pasture there he hath set me.
He nurshide me on the watir of refreischyng.
WYCLIFFE BIBLE, 1388 EDITION

The Lord is my shepherd, I shal not want.
He maketh me to rest in grene pasture
& leadeth me by the stil waters.
GENEVA BIBLE, 1560

God is my sheephearde, therfore I can lacke nothing;
he wyll cause me to repose my selfe in pasture full of grass,
and he wyll leade me vnto calme waters.
BISHOPS' BIBLE, 1568

The Lord is my shepheard, I shall not want.
He maketh me to lie downe in greene pastures:
he leadeth me beside the still waters.
KING JAMES VERSION, 1611

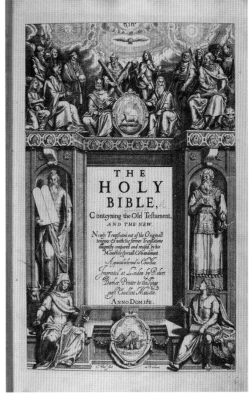

Title page of the King James Version (1611).

Slow Acceptance and Revisions

Not everyone immediately warmed to the King James Version. The Puritans especially preferred the staunchly Protestant Geneva Bible, and in 1643 printed excerpts of it in the Soldier's Pocket Bible issued to the army of Puritan leader Oliver Cromwell. And it was the Geneva Bible that many Puritans carried with them to the New World of America.

Nevertheless, by the end of the seventeenth century, the King James Version had become the Bible for English-speaking people. As Roman Catholic priest Alexander Geddes put it in 1792, "if accuracy, fidelity, and the strictest attention to the letter of the text, be supposed to constitute the qualities of an excellent version, this of all versions, must, in general, be accounted the most excellent."

The King James Version was revised in later editions, to correct mistakes, and in 1629, the first edition to be printed in Cambridge dropped the Apocrypha – a practice that caught on because it reduced printing costs. However, the first serious attempt to update the language was made with the English Revised Version (1881– 85). From this revision sprang the American Standard Version (1901), followed by the Revised Standard Version (1952) and the New Revised Standard Version (1989). Despite these re-workings, however, the original King James Version continues to be widely read and revered.

MISPRINTS

Early editions of the King James Version were plagued with misprints, which were corrected in later printings. But perhaps the most scandalous appeared in a 1631 edition, in which the printer left out an essential "not" from the seventh commandment. As a result, the Bible had God declaring that people *should* commit adultery (Exodus 20:14). This edition became known as the Wicked Bible, or the Adulterer's Bible.

Bibles in the New World

SCRIPTURE FOR INDIANS AND PURITANS

When Christopher Columbus discovered a "New World" in 1492, he determined to Christianize the local people, whom he called Indians. Consequently, on his second voyage, in 1493, Columbus brought along a Benedictine monk and five priests to evangelize the Indians. Most of the European explorers who followed Columbus to various parts of the New World followed suit.

Later, when Europeans began to settle in the New World, they brought their Bibles with them. Some even developed Bibles for their neighbours, the Indians.

Dominican friars baptize Indian converts.

A mission church near Mexico's Copper Canyon, built in 1680.

Missionaries in the New World

Beginning in 1524, after the Aztecs of Mexico had been forcibly converted by Hernán Cortéz, a group of Franciscan missionaries, known as the Twelve Apostles, established almost 400 missions in Mexico and eventually built thousands of churches there. In 1539, they set up a printing press – probably the first in the New World – and produced catechisms and other texts – but no Bibles. After Spain's Francisco Pizarro overthrew the Incas of Peru in the 1530s, missionaries moved in to convert the Incas and established the first university in the Americas at Lima.

Starting in 1549, Portuguese Jesuits established missions in hostile interior regions of Brazil. In 1568 Spanish Jesuits set up disciplined Christian villages for the Indians in Paraguay. Although they did not provide Bibles, all these missionaries passed on biblical material by word of mouth, as in the earliest times.

The Dutch settled in Guiana in 1580, followed by the French and English. The Dutch also settled in the West Indies and in New Netherlands (now New York State), where they established the Dutch Reformed Church. They

BIBLICAL PRIMERS

Americans often used primers based on the Bible to teach their children how to read. For each letter of the alphabet, these primers featured a rhymed verse on a biblical topic and a simple illustration. The verse for the letter "A" was "With Adam's fall, we sinned all." More advanced schoolbooks also told Bible stories, and in the eighteenth century girls often copied verses from the Bible in needlework.

> *O that I could address the Indians in their own language! My ardent soul longs to be sounding salvation in the ears of these red men.*
>
> JASON LEE, MISSIONARY TO OREGON

worked with the Indians in New Netherlands until the English took over the missions early in the eighteenth century.

French and Spanish explorers brought missionaries to various other parts of North America and established missions in Florida, Texas, the Mississippi River Valley, and the south-west. In 1615 missionaries from the French Order of Récollets tried to Christianize the Indians of Quebec, Canada, but remained aloof and ineffectual. In 1625 French Jesuits moved into Quebec and adopted some of the ways of the Indians, teaching them gospel values through preaching and example. They succeeded in part, but many Indians held on to their old beliefs.

Bibles in the English Colonies

The English Puritans who settled in Massachusetts in the early seventeenth century brought their Bibles with them. The earliest preferred the Geneva Bible, but by 1700 they were all using the King James Version, which had become England's official Protestant Bible. But because the King James Version was copyrighted and could only be printed by the King's Printer, the Puritans had to import their Bibles.

When Harvard College was established in 1636, a printing press was set up there. To initiate the press, three scholars – Richard Mather, John Eliot, and Thomas Weld – made a fresh translation of the Psalms from the Hebrew. And so *The Whole Booke of Psalmes Faithfully Translated into English Metre* (The Bay Psalm Book) was printed in 1640.

The first full Bible to be printed in North America was in an Algonquin Indian dialect. It was prepared by the missionary John Eliot in the Massachusetts Bay Indians' own dialect, Massachusett. Because Massachusett had never been written down, Eliot had to begin by devising a writing system.

In making his translation, Eliot did all he could to make the text understandable to the Indians. For example, he transformed the parable of the ten virgins (Matthew 25:1–12) into the parable of ten chaste men, because the Indians considered chastity to be a virtue required of men but not of women. The New Testament appeared in 1661, and the entire Bible in 1663.

In the years that followed, Scripture was translated into various other American Indian dialects, but no Bibles were published in the colonies in European languages until 1743. Then, Christopher Sauer, a German Baptist, published an edition of Luther's Bible on the outskirts of Philadelphia. When the American Revolution broke out, American printers considered their ties with England broken and began printing the King James Version. In the newly formed United States, Bibles in various translations were freely published.

JOHN ELIOT, APOSTLE TO THE INDIANS

John Eliot was born in England in 1604 and educated at Cambridge. In 1631 he sailed to Boston and soon became pastor of a church in nearby Roxbury. Eliot began preaching to the local Indians, and in 1650 he convinced some Indians to move into a new "praying town", where they built and lived in European-style houses and followed a biblical code of laws. Eliot supplied the Indians with food and clothing, while they farmed and studied English, crafts, and the Bible. When they were ready, they were baptized.

Meanwhile, back in England, admirers of Eliot's work formed a new organization to help finance his efforts. This Company for Propagating the Gospel in New England and Parts Adjacent in North America was the first of many missionary societies.

In 1654 Eliot published a catechism in the language of the Indians under his care. He followed this in 1658 with his translation of the entire Bible.

By 1674 Eliot had established 14 "praying towns", housing some 4,000 Indians. But the following year, war broke out between the colonists and the Indians, and Eliot's Indians were persecuted by both sides and nearly wiped out. Eliot later tried to revive the towns, but without his former success. He died in 1690.

Eliot preaching to Algonquin Indians.

The Bible Reviled and Exalted

THE ENLIGHTENMENT AND BEYOND

During the period known as the Enlightenment, human reason was elevated above everything else. Acknowledging that the universe was governed by natural laws, eighteenth-century thinkers concluded that by studying those laws they could come to understand the workings of nature through reason. Some concluded that even God must abide by natural law. Others regarded the Bible as fiction. Many faithful Christians rebelled at such ideas and countered them with Pietism, so the nineteenth century enjoyed a renewed interest in the Bible.

John Wesley (1703–91), the founder of Methodism, preaching while standing on his father's tomb. Wesley's Holy Club focused on Bible reading as a way to deepen personal faith.

Enlightenment Dims the Bible

Even those who did not reject the Bible altogether asked questions. First, they questioned the miracles in the Bible and tried to explain them away as literary devices or exaggerations of natural phenomena. For example, the manna in the wilderness was not bread from heaven but a sugary substance excreted by desert insects. Prophecies were also questioned, as were the stories in Genesis. Geologists held that the earth was far older than indicated by the Bible and that living creatures had appeared on earth over a vast period of time; they were not created in a single day, as described in Genesis. Consequently, it was suggested that the Genesis account was a myth and not historical. This elicited a huge cry of protest from traditional Christians.

Devotional Approaches to the Bible

In Germany, reaction against the rationalist treatment of the Bible led to a spread of Pietism. This movement had been introduced in 1677 when Lutheran minister Phillip Jacob Spener called for an intensified study of Scripture to enhance personal piety. During the Enlightenment, Pietism spread across Europe and into America.

In England, between 1708 and 1712, the Presbyterian minister Matthew Henry published Bible commentaries that were personally meaningful. In them, Henry sought to provide the reader with biblical ideas and images that gave meaning to his or her individual life. Henry's approach was adopted by John Wesley in his *Notes on the New Testament*, published in 1754 and 1765.

To bring these ideas to the people, small study groups appeared throughout the Western world. At Oxford, in 1729, John Wesley organized the Holy Club, whose members sought to deepen their faith by intensive Bible reading.

In the American colonies, between 1720 and 1740, a religious movement known as the Great Awakening spread across the land. Addressing crowds that were so large they had to meet in open fields, the preacher George Whitefield brought out the emotions of his audiences, stressing the "terrors of the law" to sinners and "new birth" in Jesus Christ. At the same time, Jonathan Edwards, a Congregationalist preacher, attempted to help Christians to separate the true works of the Spirit of God from the false.

In music, both Johann Sebastian Bach and Georg Friedrich Handel composed cantatas and oratorios based on biblical subjects. These included choruses and emotional arias that emphasized personal piety. Handel's *Messiah* is still a perennial favourite, including the famous "Hallelujah Chorus".

Jonathan Edwards (1703–58) emerged a champion of evangelical religion in America's Great Awakening.

Have courage to use your own reason.

IMMANUEL KANT

● SEE ALSO
THE BIBLE AND LITERATURE, PP. 116–17
THE BIBLE ON STAGE AND SCREEN,
PP. 118–19

JEHOVAH'S WITNESSES

The worldwide movement now known as Jehovah's Witnesses was formed in the 1880s by the American lay preacher Charles Taze Russell. Russell claimed that Jesus Christ, a perfect man, had returned invisibly to earth in 1878 to prepare for the kingdom of God, which would be inaugurated after the battle of Armageddon in 1914. Russell urged everyone to study the Bible and to warn as many people as possible of the impending end of time. When Armageddon didn't materialize as predicted, the prophecies were reinterpreted. Russell died in 1916 and his successor, J.F. Rutherford, turned the movement into a "theocratic" one, dedicated to the truth and demanding the full commitment of its members. The movement has its own translations of the Bible, which reinforce its emphasis on preparing for the end time.

Charles Taze Russell (1852–1916), founder of the Jehovah's Witnesses.

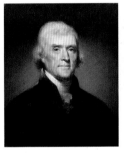

While serving as president of the United States, Thomas Jefferson (1743–1826) put together his own unique version of the Gospels. Shown here in a portrait by Rembrandt Peale.

Elizabeth Cady Stanton (1815–1902), an American women's suffrage leader, helped produce *The Woman's Bible*.

Joseph Smith has a vision of the angel Moroni delivering a long-lost book to him. Smith's vision led him to found the Mormons.

Nineteenth-Century Bibles

By the start of the nineteenth century, Scripture had been translated into 48 European languages, but a few new translations appeared later, as well as some interesting side products, as follows:

■ The first Scottish Bible (in Gaelic) was published in 1801.

■ Unitarians, who reject the doctrine of the Trinity and the divinity of Jesus, published various "corrected" versions of the Bible.

■ In 1803, US president Thomas Jefferson created his own version of the Gospels by collecting passages that presented Jesus' "true message" in English, Greek, Latin, and French.

■ Joseph Smith, a young American, said he had a vision of the angel Moroni, who showed him a long-lost book that told about Jesus' visit to North America just after his resurrection, to advise a group of Israelites who had fled there to escape the Babylonians in 586 BC. In 1830, Smith published the text. The Book of Mormon still serves as scripture for Smith's Church of Jesus Christ of Latter-Day Saints (the Mormons).

■ Family Bibles emerged, with pages for entering births, baptisms, marriages, and deaths.

■ The first Bible in Hebrew to be printed in the United States appeared in 1814.

■ In 1836, the New York Asylum for the Blind issued a New Testament with raised letters. This appeared almost 20 years before the development of the Braille system.

■ In 1895–98, Elizabeth Cady Stanton and other women's rights activists published *The Woman's Bible*, consisting of Bible excerpts, together with feminist commentaries.

To the Ends of the Earth

GOOD NEWS FOR THE FAR EAST AND THE SOUTH SEAS

Jesus' last command to his apostles was: "be my witnesses... *to the ends of the earth*" (Acts 1:8). More than 14 centuries later, the ends of the earth suddenly became far more distant, when reports came back to Europe from Columbus and other explorers of rich new worlds filled with peoples who had no knowledge of Jesus. In response, ambitious Christians reached out to these souls either individually or through missionary societies. They all had one ambition – to Christianize the world, including both the known and unknown lands in the Far East and the South Seas.

Early Efforts in the Orient

According to legend the apostle Thomas took the good news to India. Subsequently, the Italian Franciscan John of Montecorvino and two companions preached about Jesus in Madras in 1291. With other Franciscans John then went to Beijing, where he established a Christian community and translated the Bible into Uighur, the language of the Mongol ruling class. He was named bishop of Beijing in 1307, but his community did not survive the fall of the Mongol dynasty later in the century.

In April 1541 Francis Xavier, a Jesuit missionary, sailed to Portugal's new colony in western India. Working among fishermen and pearl divers, he converted thousands. In 1549 Xavier moved on to Japan, studied the language, translated a catechism, and made many converts. On his way to China, he died. Unfortunately, without a Bible, the people of India and Japan understood Christianity poorly. When Xavier died, their faith languished.

In 1582 another Jesuit, Matteo Ricci, sailed to China. To reach the people, who were suspicious of foreigners, Ricci came up with a mission strategy that is still used today: he tried to fit in with the local culture. He wore the robes of a Confucian scholar, wrote a Chinese catechism, and conducted Mass in Chinese.

Later Efforts in the Orient

By the late eighteenth century, dozens of Protestant missionary societies were at work from Britain, France, Germany, and Belgium. Two individual missionaries from this period stand out. The first was an English apprentice shoemaker named William Carey. When he failed at leatherworking, his employer financed his study of languages. In 1793 the newly formed Baptist Missionary Society sent Carey to India, where he translated the entire Bible

Spanish priest Francis Xavier takes the gospel to India. Scene from "The Miracles of St Francis Xavier".

into 6 Indian dialects and parts of the Bible into 29 other languages.

The other outstanding missionary was the Englishman Hudson Taylor, who travelled through China wearing Chinese clothes and toting a bag of Chinese Bibles. After seven years in China, Taylor returned to England, where he translated the Bible into Chinese dialects and recruited missionaries. In 1865 he set up the China Inland Mission (now called the Overseas Missionary Fellowship International) to continue his work.

When the Boxer Rebellion broke out in 1900 the Chinese reacted against abusive foreign trading treaties by killing foreigners and 30,000 Chinese Christians. The uprising was quelled, but Chinese resentment continued to build for another 50 years, until the communists expelled all "foreign devils". Christians responded by smuggling Bibles into China. Today the Chinese are more tolerant and even publish the Bible in Chinese.

Italian priest Matteo Ricci, dressed as a Confucian scholar.

● SEE ALSO
A BIBLE IN EVERY HOME,
PP. 104–105

> *We prepared to go ashore to publish for the first time in New Zealand the glad tidings of the gospel.*
>
> SAMUEL MARSDEN

Mixed Results in the South Seas

Meanwhile, other missionaries were heading south. In 1795, on hearing that the South Sea islanders were heathen cannibals, British preacher Thomas Haweis organized the London Missionary Society to spread the gospel among them. In 1796 the society sent out a team of 4 ministers and 26 skilled craftsmen with their wives and children. More than half the team went to Tahiti. The others sailed to the neighbouring islands of the Marquesas and Tonga, where some were murdered and none were successful.

On Tahiti, however, the missionaries made progress. The bricklayer Henry Nott created a written language based on phonetics. With this, and the help of King Pomare II, who said, "I want to learn the talking marks," the missionaries started translating the Bible. Since one of the missionaries was a printer who had brought his press, he printed the Bible in sections, as it was translated.

Wooing the Cannibals

English minister Samuel Marsden, chaplain to the Australian settlement of British convicts, decided to take the gospel to New Zealand, to convert the Maoris, who had a reputation for killing and eating visitors. Ignoring the advice of everyone he knew, he bought a ship and with the help of a New Zealander he had once nursed back to health, Marsden sailed to New Zealand in 1814. On Christmas Day, Marsden preached New Zealand's first Christian sermon, using his friend as a translator.

After returning home, Marsden sent back missionaries, who gradually created a written language for the Maori and translated Bible passages. It took 40 years before an entire Bible was published.

Welcome in Hawaii

The American Board of Commissioners of Foreign Missions sent missionaries to Hawaii in 1820. When one of the missionary's wives nursed Queen Kaahumanu back to health from a serious illness, the queen converted, as did all her subjects. Some 10 years later more than 50,000 Hawaiians were enrolled in missionary schools, where they learned to read and studied the Bible.

As elsewhere, the missionaries had developed a written language. Over a period of 20 years they translated the entire Bible. The Hawaiian Bible's story of creation sounded much like a local legend: the gods "formed man out of the red earth and breathed into his nose, and he became a living being".

Samuel Marsden and his fellow missionary John Liddlard Nicholas meet native Maoris in New Zealand.

Doomsday Specialists

AWAITING THE END OF THE WORLD

The Bible says human history will end one day. Jesus said the date of the apocalypse is something "no one knows… only the Father" (Matthew 24:36). Yet Christians insist on searching for clues, sifting mainly through perplexing passages in Revelation, Daniel, and Ezekiel – passages traditionally thought to poetically symbolize the ongoing war between good and evil, or perhaps to serve as coded messages of comfort in times of crisis.

When Jesus' disciples asked when the end was coming, Jesus said that certain signs would signal the beginning of the end: famines and earthquakes, wars and rumours of wars and false messiahs. Christians keep trying to find and interpret these signs in order to do what Jesus said they could not do – predict the Day of Doom. Many have tried and all have failed. More will try again.

Medieval Predictions

Apocalyptic fever had its first major outbreak on the eve of the first millennium, creating a wave of paranoia that lasted for centuries. To support their predictions of the end times, clergy pointed to comets, eclipses, wars, earthquakes, and – in later times – the Black Death.

One person who especially drove up the apocalyptic fever was the Italian monk Joachim of Fiore (c.1132–1202), who divided history into three overlapping eras, one for each member of the Trinity. The Old Testament was the time of the Father. The New Testament was the time of the Son. Yet to come was the utopian era of the Holy Spirit, which Joachim said would begin between 1200 and 1260 and end with the coming of the Antichrist, the epitome of evil. Joachim said the seven-headed dragon of Revelation 12 represented seven leaders. He added that Saladin – the Muslim leader who had captured Jerusalem from the crusaders in 1187 – was the sixth head and that the Antichrist would be the seventh.

Calculating and Recalculating the End Time

One of the many to have calculated the end of the world in more recent times was William Miller, a New England farmer-turned-lecturer. By linking cryptic numbers in the books of Daniel and Revelation and subjecting them to mathematical calculations, Miller concluded that the world would end in 1843. When it did not, he recalculated and changed the date to 1844. When this prediction also failed, many of his followers left what was called the "Adventist" movement (from a word meaning "to come"). When Miller died, some of his lingering followers founded the Seventh-day Adventist Church.

Representation of the seven-headed dragon from Joachim of Fiore's *Book of Figures*.

Apocalyptic fever also affected art, as in this detail from "Damned in Hell", part of the Last Judgement fresco cycle by Luca Signorelli (c.1441–1523). Fresco from Capella Nuova, Orvieto Cathedral, Italy.

Deliberate Frauds

Other predictions were deliberate swindles. Jang Rim Lee, a South Korean preacher, started a wave of end-time hysteria in 1987, when he predicted a 1992 rapture in which Jesus would sweep out of the sky and take the godly home. Some 100,000 people followed Lee and millions more tracked the events in news reports. Then nothing happened, but Lee had collected over 4 million dollars in donations, much of which he invested in bonds that matured in May 1993. He was imprisoned for fraud.

APOCALYPTIC SIGNS AND PREDICTIONS

- **1945**: Atomic bomb falls on Hiroshima, reminding Christians that "The day of the Lord will come like a thief… the elements will be dissolved with fire" (2 Peter 3:10).

- **1993**: A standoff in Waco, Texas, between federal agents and the Branch Davidians, an end-time cult led by David Koresh, results in the death of some 80 cult members. Koresh had taught that the US government was the evil Babylon described in Revelation.

- **1997**: Thirty-nine members of the Heaven's Gate cult commit suicide in a California mansion. They believed a spaceship was travelling behind the Hale-Bopp comet, and that they could leave their physical bodies and ascend to an extraterrestrial "Kingdom of Heaven".

- **2012**: Many Christians seriously believe that an entry in an ancient Mayan calendar accurately predicted the destruction of the earth in December 2012, though Mayan scholars dismissed such an interpretation of the ancient text.

Dispensationalism

Soon after, British theologian John Nelson Darby preached Dispensationalism, in which history is divided into eras, or dispensations – such as the era of law (Moses to Jesus). Darby drew up a scenario in which the first scene is the rapture, when Christians are taken to heaven. For those left behind, seven years of tribulation follow, led by the Antichrist. Next, a northern army invades the Middle East, starting the battle of Armageddon. Jesus returns, destroys the Antichrist, restores the temple, and rules for a millennium. Then comes Judgment Day.

British theologian John Nelson Darby (1800–82) taught that this "dispensation", or era, in human history is the last one, and the end could come at any instant.

Late Great Planet

In 1970 a campus preacher named Hal Lindsey popularized Darby's theology in *The Late Great Planet Earth*, a best-selling book that linked contemporary events to ancient prophecy. The Bible predicted fervent heat would decimate the planet (2 Peter 3:10), and nuclear bombs can now accomplish that. The Bible said the entire world would see the dead bodies of two end-time martyrs (Revelation 11:7–9), and satellites can now broadcast such images worldwide. The Bible said Israel would be restored, and Israel re-emerged in 1948 as a sovereign nation.

Lindsey predicted that the rapture of Christians into heaven would occur by 1988 – within a 40-year generation of Israel's emergence as a nation in 1948. Lindsey based this on Jesus' teaching that the "end of the age" would come before "this generation" was over (Matthew 24:34). Lindsey said the generation Jesus meant was the one after the rebirth of modern Israel. Nothing happened. It is thought that Jesus had probably been referring to the fall of Jerusalem in AD 70 – about 40 years after his own ministry.

A Bible in Every Home

BIBLE SOCIETIES AND WYCLIFFE BIBLE TRANSLATORS

During the nineteenth and the early twentieth centuries, it was not unusual to find travelling salesmen trekking from one place to another to sell Bibles to the local people at low prices. Travelling by foot, on bicycles, or in special vans, these Bible sellers were known as colporteurs, from the French name for hawkers who carried their goods on their backs. Colporteurs were not out for profit, but sought only to fulfil the mission of the societies they worked for – to distribute Bibles to everyone.

Missionary Tim Robinson, who works with Wycliffe UK, is seen here in Nigeria, selling Mwaghavul Scriptures.

A colporteur offers pages from the Bible to a young Cantonese in China around 1900.

Emergence of Bible Societies

On 7 March 1804, the British and Foreign Bible Society was founded when some 300 Protestant laymen met in a London tavern to discuss the place of Bible distribution in their work. Despite doctrinal differences, these Christians formed a society whose sole purpose was to print copies of Scripture "without note or comment", and to distribute them without financial gain throughout the world.

In the next 10 years, hundreds of independent and auxiliary societies sprang up in Europe, Canada, and the United States. By 1900 nearly 2,000 colporteurs were working for Bible societies in nearly all the countries of the world.

Reaching the Ends of the Earth

Because these Bible societies were committed to distributing Scripture to the ends of the earth, they needed translations, and through the years they translated Scripture into an incredible number of languages.

As the British, Dutch, and American Bible societies spread throughout the world, some overlap occurred in the areas they were serving, so in 1946, 14 European, British, and American societies joined to form the United Bible Societies, a centre for coordinating and planning the work of Bible translation and distribution in all parts of the globe. At first, the Catholic Church opposed the work of the Bible societies, preferring to have their own scholars monitor the interpretation of Scripture. In the mid twentieth century, however, Catholics began to join with the Bible societies in translating and distributing Scripture.

In 2012, the United Bible Societies incorporated 146 national societies, which were distributing upwards of 400 million Bibles – or parts of Bibles – each year.

God, who has no linguistic favourites, has determined that we should all have the good news in our native tongue.

LAMIN SANNEH, GAMBIAN THEOLOGIAN

The Wycliffe Bible Translators Are Founded

One day in the 1930s, while William Cameron Townsend was working among Guatemala's Cakchiquel Indians, a local man asked: "If your God is so great, why doesn't he speak my language?" Soon after, Townsend established a linguistics school for training future Bible translators, which he named after John Wycliffe, the first to translate the Bible into English.

Once students completed their training, Townsend sent them into the field to develop writing systems for languages that lacked them and to translate Scripture into those languages. His sole aim was to supply Bibles to peoples who had none in their own language.

A member of the Wycliffe translation team in Togo, West Africa, receives newly translated Ncham Bibles for a dedication ceremony in Bassar.

Wycliffe Bible Translators Sue Arthur and Ezekiel Rhila at work at a recent translation-checking workshop in Jos, Nigeria.

The Work of Translating

Wycliffe Bible Translators works hard to identify cultures that have no written language and then works with local native speakers to develop writing systems and translate the Bible. Projects usually start with the buy-in of the local communities and involvement of local churches, and often local translators work with other translators in neighbouring languages to translate the Bible, with the support of Wycliffe consultants.

Translating Scripture for unknown cultures is not easy. To begin with, translators must organize a way of dealing with the specific sounds of a language. Often symbols need to be found for sounds not used in European languages. These include a sound made in West Africa by flapping the lip rather than the tip of the tongue, the clicking sounds used in other African languages, and a sound made with the tongue sticking out, as used in Pirahã, a Brazilian dialect. Today, computers chart and organize sounds and find symbols to represent them.

The work of translating presents other problems, as well. It is often difficult to find an appropriate word for one used in Hebrew or Greek. For example, Isaiah's statement that our sins "shall be like snow" would be meaningless in a jungle. On the other hand, some languages contain many words with various shadings of meaning for a single Hebrew or Greek word. The Eskimos, for example, have many different words for snow. Translators must choose the right word to fit the biblical context. Finally, some languages lack words that seem essential to us. Languages in Papua New Guinea have no words for "before" or "after", requiring translators to suggest the proper sequence without being able to state it directly.

Wycliffe Bible Translators has already translated at least parts of Scripture into 500 languages. By 2025 it hopes to have translation projects started – although not necessarily completed – in every language that needs one.

GIDEON BIBLES

In America, independent of the Bible Societies, two businessmen met one night in 1898, and started an organization to distribute Bibles, naming it after the Old Testament hero Gideon. The sole purpose of the association was to "put the word of God into the hands of the unconverted". Over the years, the Gideons have placed copies of the Bible in hotel and hospital rooms, schools, and prisons around the world. By 2015, the number of copies they had placed had passed the 2 billion mark.

Ways to Translate

WORD FOR WORD OR THOUGHT FOR THOUGHT

If you were starting work on a new Bible translation, you would have one critical question to answer: How closely should I follow the ancient text? If the Hebrew text speaks of a sacrificial "lamb", should I use the same term – even if my intended readers are isolated Eskimos who have never seen a lamb? Or should I substitute "seal pup", as Wycliffe Bible Translators once did?

Translators are sharply divided over whether to narrowly follow the words and sentence structure of the ancient languages or to present the basic ideas in a way today's readers can understand. The King James Version and the New American Standard Bible followed the literal approach. Examples of less literal, or thought-for-thought, translation are the New International Version, New Revised Standard Version, and New Living Translation.

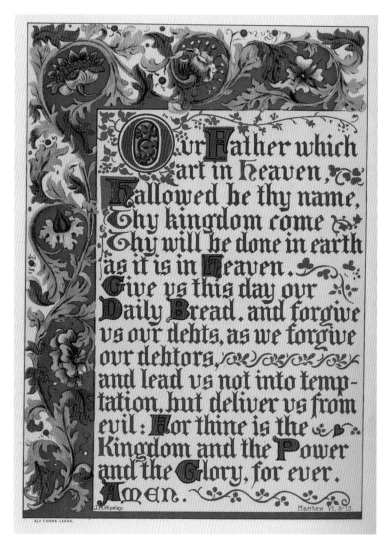

The Lord's Prayer in an ornate copy of the King James Version.

The Case for Literal Translations

Some people prefer word-for-word translations even when the English phrasing is awkward or difficult to understand. They reason that, as awkward as it is, this is what the Bible says. So highly poetic statements or obscure Hebrew sayings are kept, though they are hard to follow today. For example, the image of "heaping coals of fire" on an enemy may sound to a reader today like an approval of torture, but it is actually a highly dramatic way of saying "make enemies regret what they did". Two translations of Romans 12:20 show the basic approaches to translation. The first is a fairly literal translation, and the second is far freer:

> But if your enemy is hungry, feed him... for in so doing you will heap burning coals upon his head.

New American Standard Bible

> If your enemies are hungry, feed them... and they will be ashamed of what they have done to you.

New Living Translation

Bible students who prefer the more literal versions of Scripture acknowledge that these are harder for most people to understand. But the place to clear up the confusion, they insist, is not in the Bible text, but in marginal notes or in commentaries and dictionaries. This approach also helps to keep translators from weaving their own theological preferences into the text.

Translation it is that opens the window, to let in the light; that breaks the shell, that we might eat the kernel.

KING JAMES VERSION TRANSLATORS

The Case for Freer Translations

There are serious problems with trying to translate ancient languages, word for word, into modern languages. To begin with, it is impossible to reproduce the rhythm, puns, word sounds, and other literary devices that beef up the message in the original language. In addition, there are often no matching words or there are words that have multiple meanings and it is difficult to tell which meaning pertains in a given passage. For example, the Hebrew word *hesed* can mean devotion, love, kindness, goodness, grace, mercy, or loyalty. Some translators say it is best to pick one word and use it throughout a translation. Others say the context of the passage should determine which word to use.

In the mid twentieth century scholars started to argue that the most important job of Bible translators is not to preserve the literary structure of Scripture, but to communicate clearly what it means. So instead of trying to translate word for word, they translated thought for thought. "As literal as possible, as free as necessary" were the guiding words for the translators working on the New Revised Standard Version published in 1989.

Some Bibles, such as *The Message*, are so freely rendered that scholars call them paraphrases, not translations. In preparing such versions the translators focus on the target audience to determine how literal or free to make a translation. For example, if the intended readers are newcomers to the Bible, the translator may substitute words like "goodness" and "devotion" for such longstanding biblical terms as "righteousness" and "sanctification". But if the intended audience is biblically literate, they may keep traditional terms.

Most scholars maintain there is no one right way to translate the Bible. For today's translator, the challenge is to find a balance between accuracy and readability.

TRANSLATING THE LORD'S PRAYER

Differences between translations can be subtle or extreme. Here are samples of how several versions translate the second half of the Lord's Prayer (Matthew 6:11–13). The examples are listed in order from the more literal translations to the most free.

YOUNG'S LITERAL TRANSLATION, 1898

Our appointed bread give us to-day.
And forgive us our debts, as also we forgive our debtors.
And mayest Thou not lead us to temptation, but deliver us from the evil.

NEW AMERICAN STANDARD BIBLE, REVISED 1995

Give us this day our daily bread.
And forgive us our debts, as we also have forgiven our debtors.
And do not lead us into temptation, but deliver us from evil.

KING JAMES VERSION, 1611

Give us this day our daily bread.
And forgive us our debts, as we forgive our debtors.
And lead us not into temptation, but deliver us from evil.

NEW REVISED STANDARD VERSION, 1989

Give us this day our daily bread.
And forgive us our debts, as we also have forgiven our debtors.
And do not bring us to the time of trial, but rescue us from the evil one.

NEW INTERNATIONAL VERSION, REVISED 1984

Give us today our daily bread.
Forgive us our debts,
as we also have forgiven our debtors.
And lead us not into temptation,
but deliver us from the evil one.

NEW AMERICAN BIBLE, REVISED 1986

Give us today our daily bread;
and forgive us our debts, as we forgive our debtors;
and do not subject us to the final test,
but deliver us from the evil one.

NEW LIVING TRANSLATION, 1996

Give us our food for today,
and forgive us our sins,
just as we have forgiven those who have sinned against us.
And don't let us yield to temptation,
but deliver us from the evil one.

THE MESSAGE, 1993

Keep us alive with three square meals.
Keep us forgiven with you and forgiving others.
Keep us safe from ourselves and the Devil.
You're in charge!
You can do anything you want!
You're ablaze in beauty!
Yes. Yes. Yes.

MODELS FOR INTERNATIONAL TRANSLATIONS

Two Bibles have served as translation models around the world. People wanting a conversational tone translated from the English-language Good News Bible. People wanting a more literal tone translated from the French Jerusalem Bible. These two approaches have shown up in German, Italian, Spanish, and many other languages.

Digging Up the Past

ARCHAEOLOGISTS AND THE DEAD SEA SCROLLS

Bible scholars began to turn to archaeology about 200 years ago. Inspired by digs at Stonehenge and ancient Troy, they began to look at sites in the Bible lands to bring new light to the Bible and establish the authenticity of its contents. They examined artefacts and writings from biblical times and came to discover that secrets of the past were buried under large mounds, or tells, that look like gently rolling hills but actually cover layer upon layer of past civilizations. By digging into these tells they uncovered a wealth of information about Bible times. Along the shores of the Dead Sea they also discovered the oldest surviving copies of Old Testament texts.

Archaeologist Sir Flinders Petrie (1853–1942) arranges pottery he found in southern Palestine.

The Temple Scroll, which outlines plans for a new ideal Jewish temple.

Biblical Archaeology

Biblical archaeology began seriously in 1890, when British scholar W.M. Flinders Petrie dug up a mound near Jerusalem and found layers of past villages built one on top of the other. Petrie also began matching pottery styles with particular time periods, allowing him to estimate when certain biblical events occurred – a practice still used today.

At first archaeologists sought out sites mentioned in the Bible, hoping to authenticate biblical accounts. But starting with preconceived notions – such as hoping that a mound covered a particular site – led archaeologists to jump to wrong conclusions. So today, instead of bringing their own theories to a site, they let the site speak for itself. To interpret what they dig up, archaeologists rely on geologists, linguists, climatologists, anthropologists, zoologists, engineers, computer programmers, and biblical scholars.

In the last few decades, archaeologists have unearthed weapons of war, peace treaties, a first-century fishing boat, and a burial box bearing the name of Caiaphas, the high priest who tried Jesus. They have also uncovered and deciphered entire libraries. Mainly, however, archaeologists carefully sift through materials ranging from bones to pollen, searching for clues to what life was like in Bible times.

The Dead Sea Scrolls

The most important archaeological find in the history of the Bible began in the winter of 1946–47, when a young shepherd explored a cave in the cliffs near the Dead Sea and found three scrolls inside clay pots. Archaeologists subsequently scoured nearby caves and discovered a library of Jewish writings dating from about 250 BC to AD 68 – when Roman soldiers overran the community that owned the library.

Scattered among 11 caves were remnants of some 800 manuscripts, about 200 of which were copies of Old Testament books. Only about a dozen manuscripts were intact. The rest lay in crumbled scraps. Scholars are still trying to piece them together.

The interior of cave four at Qumran, in which 15,000 scroll fragments have been found.

SPACE-AGE HELP

Some ink on the Dead Sea Scrolls has faded so much that the letters cannot be seen by the naked eye, but show up clearly when photographed by infrared-sensitive film. This film was pioneered by the space programme as a way to photograph the earth using cameras in orbit.

DNA testing is also used on parchment scrolls, as they are made from animal skins. Analysis allows scientists to pinpoint which scraps of parchment came from the same animal – and consequently the same scroll.

There are three distinct kinds of writing in the Dead Sea Scrolls:

■ General religious writings, such as prayer books and biblical commentaries, which focus on the end times, when God will conquer sin and set up a righteous kingdom. The scrolls warned that the end was near and that the community members were the "Sons of Light" who would soon ride with God's army to defeat the "Sons of Darkness" (the Romans and other sinful people).

■ Rules to live by for members of the community, which outline rites that keep the "Sons of Light" pure enough to fight in God's army. A war scroll seems to contain a battle plan for that war.

■ Copies of Old Testament books include a complete Isaiah scroll and at least parts of every book in the Old Testament except Esther. Remarkably, these copies are almost identical to the traditional Masoretic text produced a millennium later. There are, however, some differences. For example, one scroll puts the psalms in an unusual order and includes three previously unknown psalms.

THE QUMRAN COMMUNITY

Most Bible scholars believe the Dead Sea Scrolls are the work of a group of monk-like Jewish men called Essenes ("pious ones"), who, like the Pharisees and the Sadducees, formed a distinct branch of the Jewish faith.

In about 152 BC, when a Jewish leader in Israel's war of independence from Syria declared himself the new high priest, the Essenes severed all ties with other Jews. Some moved to Qumran, a tiny walled village in the desert near the Dead Sea, taking with them the sacred Jewish writings they had preserved by copying. Leaders in the group added new works, such as predictions about the approaching end times. Ironically, what came was the end of their community. Roman soldiers crushing a nationwide Jewish rebellion decimated the settlement in AD 68. Forewarned of the attack, the Essenes hid the scrolls in the nearby caves, where they remained until the late 1940s.

A fragment of the so-called Copper Scroll, inscribed on a sheet of copper. The Hebrew text contains sketchy directions to buried treasure.

Biblical Criticism Emerges

INVESTIGATING TEXTS, SOURCES, AND AUTHORS

Biblical scholars were exhilarated by the discovery of the Old Testament texts among the Dead Sea Scrolls. These manuscripts are far older than any other surviving copies, and they spurred scholars to study the basic elements of the biblical texts more closely than ever. This gave new vigour to the field of study known as biblical criticism, which had come to full maturity in the early twentieth century.

Early biblical criticism had two basic aims. First, to identify the Bible's authors and their sources to get a better grasp of what they meant to communicate to their first readers. Second, to establish biblical texts that are error-free and as close as possible to the original texts. The Dead Sea Scrolls help fulfil both of the aims of biblical criticism.

STANDARD BIBLICAL TEXTS

Before studying a biblical work closely – and especially before translating one – scholars choose a single ancient text as their main source, though they also consult other versions and even other translations as they proceed. Most translators use the following versions:

- For the Old Testament, The *Biblia Hebraica Stuttgartensis*, first published in Stuttgart, Germany, in 1966–77. The biblical text is that of the *Leningrad Codex*, which dates to 1010, making it the oldest complete Hebrew Bible in existence, but it also incorporates notes on variant readings, including some from the Dead Sea Scrolls.

- For the New Testament, the fifth edition of *The Greek New Testament*, published in 2014. This version includes a basic text plus evaluations of readings that differ from it in various early manuscripts, citations from the church fathers and various ancient translations.

Differences in the number of animals Noah took aboard the ark led scholars to believe Genesis had more than one author.

Authors and Sources

Scholars had long questioned traditions about certain biblical books, such as the belief that David had written all the psalms, even Psalm 137, which was composed in Babylon centuries after David's death. But in the nineteenth century scholars began to look more critically at such puzzlers as why there are two versions of the flood story in Genesis. Then, in 1878, Julius Wellhausen formulated the Documentary Hypothesis, which holds that the Pentateuch was made up of four distinct narratives that were united during the Babylonian captivity.

New Testament books were also scrutinized. Scholars speculated that some of the letters attributed to Paul were not his. Others indicated that Mark's Gospel was written first and Matthew and Luke copied it, adding material of their own. In short, scholars questioned everything – not to discredit Scripture, but to clarify the biblical books by looking into the history of their composition.

● SEE ALSO
SHAPING THE PENTATEUCH,
PP. 16–17
BREAKING DOWN THE BIBLICAL TEXTS,
PP. 112–13

The task of text criticism is to scrutinize all variant readings throughout the history of the text, and to separate the true variants from the pseudo-variants... Pseudo variants arise from early attempts to update the text and make it understandable to a specific community, or from unintentional errors in copying.

JAMES A. SANDERS, TEXTUAL CRITIC

Variants

Scholars also used variants in different versions of the Bible to recover the original texts. Studying variants from the official texts in the Dead Sea Scrolls and the Septuagint (early Greek translation) made it clear that Old Testament texts were often revised up until the time the Jewish biblical canon was set and held to be unchangeable – soon after AD 70. Scholars now use these variants to help reconstruct the history of the biblical books, from original writing through revisions, to establish which versions are the most authentic.

In practice, when faced with a questionable reading in the standard text, scholars consult other ancient versions of the Scriptures, such as the Dead Sea Scrolls, and look at early translations of these passages. They then decide whether to use the problematic text or to emend, or correct, it.

A classic problem involving variants concerns the Ten Commandments. In Exodus 20:11, the reason given to remember the Sabbath is that God created the universe in six days and rested on the seventh day, blessing and consecrating that day. In Deuteronomy 5:15, the reason is to serve as a reminder that the Lord had delivered the Israelites from slavery in Egypt. In a version of Deuteronomy found among the Dead Sea Scrolls, both reasons are given. Scholars must decide which is the earliest and truest reason.

This coloured woodcut by Julius Schnorr von Carolsfield (1794–1874) shows God resting on the Sabbath, the seventh day, having created the universe in six days. Exodus 20:11 cites this as a reason to observe the Sabbath, but other passages differ. Textual critics study such variants for legitimacy.

Some scholars maintain that Paul did not write the New Testament's letters to Timothy, although Timothy is pictured with the letter-writing Paul in this fifteenth-century illumination.

DEALING WITH VARIANTS

Over the years textual critics have developed general guidelines to help them establish the accuracy of biblical texts, although discretion must be used in applying them:

1. The shorter the reading, the more likely it is to be the original. Scribes often added material for clarification, but seldom deleted any text – it was sacred.

2. The more difficult the reading, the more likely it is to be the original. Scribes often simplified texts to clarify them, but were unlikely to muddy the readings.

3. For questionable words look for substitutions that sound or look alike: they may be scribal errors.

4. Watch for passages a scribe may have skipped by jumping a line or going from one use of a word to a later use of the same word.

5. As a last resort, substitute a similar word for a puzzling one. For example, Amos 6:12 translates as "Does one plough in the mornings?" By changing the word *babbeqarim* to *bebaqar* the verse can be translated as "Does one plough the sea with oxen?"

Breaking Down the Biblical Texts

FORM CRITICISM AND REDACTION CRITICISM

At the start of the twentieth century a new type of historic criticism, known as form criticism, became popular. Its purpose was to study the literary forms, or genres, found in the Bible in order to better understand what the biblical authors meant to convey to their first readers. But form criticism focused only on small parts of a biblical book, so later scholars concentrated on how these units were assembled and reworked at later times by people called redactors.

Studies of the psalms show that they were written over a long time span, and therefore not all of them could have been written by King David, who is shown here in an illustration from a twelfth-century psalter.

Form Criticism and the Old Testament

In 1901 Hermann Gunkel separated units of early traditions found in Genesis from material added later and studied the literary forms in which particular thoughts had been expressed. He then divided the text into types of form, such as genealogies, miracle stories, songs, and folk tales.

When biblical stories were still being handed on by word of mouth, these forms were developed to help trigger the teller's memory and the listener's recognition. A certain type of story, therefore, followed a particular pattern.

In order to determine the literary form of a passage, Gunkel held, it was necessary to delve into the *Sitz im Leben* that gave rise to it. By *Sitz im Leben* Gunkel meant all circumstances relating to the telling, writing, and developing of a story. What type of person was passing on the story? To whom was he transmitting it? What was going on historically? Was it a time of war or peace, famine or prosperity? What literary forms were prevalent? Such circumstances, Gunkel believed, influenced how a storyteller shaped his material.

After collecting this information, Gunkel traced the progress of the stories from their oral origins to their development into groups of stories and ultimately into the form in which they appear today.

In studying the psalms, Gunkel focused on their literary characteristics and historical development. He classified the individual psalms into standard types, including psalms of praise, thanksgiving, and lament. He then analysed each type. For example, he found that most laments contained common elements: a summons in the name of Yahweh and a call for help, the complaint itself, a petition, a statement of confidence in God, and a promise to praise God.

Seeing that, in sacred scripture, God speaks through men in human fashion, it follows that the human interpreter… should carefully search out the meaning which the sacred writers really had in mind.

SECOND VATICAN COUNCIL

Form Criticism of the New Testament

In 1921 Rudolf Bultmann applied form criticism to the Gospels, classifying stories about Jesus into sayings, miracle stories, and infancy, passion, and Easter narratives. He then further divided these types into subtypes and even sub-subtypes.

Bultmann and others held that these types were often influenced by the needs of the early church and were developed in three stages, reflecting:

■ The *Sitz im Leben*, or situation in the life, of Jesus.

■ The situation in the life of the early church (how Jesus' followers shaped the events they had witnessed to suit what was currently happening in the church).

■ The situation in the life of the evangelist, who shaped materials to suit his first readers.

The form critic pared away the influences of the second and third of these stages to arrive at a more exact representation of the words and deeds of Jesus.

Redaction criticism was first used in a study of the story of Jesus calming the storm, shown here in a 1695 painting by Ludolf Backhuysen (1631–1708).

Redaction Criticism of the Gospels

Form criticism focused on small units and how they were initiated and reworked. Scholars called both those who first put two or more traditions together and those who revised such accounts redactors. In the 1950s scholars started seeking the intentions of redactors and the theological emphases they may have placed on the biblical traditions.

In 1948 Gunther Bornkamm showed how Matthew took the account of Jesus quieting the storm from Mark and gave it a new meaning. Mark, Bornkamm held, used the story to demonstrate Jesus' power over nature. Matthew used it to show Jesus as the "Messiah of deed" after having shown him as the "Messiah of the word" in the Sermon on the Mount. Bornkamm later applied redaction criticism to Jesus' discourses, bringing out Matthew's ideas on the church and its relationship to the second coming of Jesus.

In 1953 Hans Conzelmann went through the Gospel of Luke, separating Luke's own editorial material from his sources. In the past, Luke had been seen as a mere chronicler of events, but Conzelmann showed that Luke was much more a theologian. Even time and geography have theological purposes in Luke, who divides time into three major periods: the period of Israel, the period of Jesus' ministry, and the period from Jesus' ascension to his second coming. Luke used this time frame and other tools to explain the delay in the second coming, which seemed past due.

In 1956–59, Willi Marxsen, the first to use the term "redaction criticism", investigated the *Sitz im Leben* of Mark's Gospel to establish the evangelist's purpose and point of view. He focused mainly on Mark's treatment of John the Baptist, geography, the concept of gospel, and the end times.

Redaction Criticism of the Old Testament

Scholars also used redaction criticism to study the Old Testament. Some studied the redactors of the prophets, concluding that the prophetic books went through various revisions before arriving at the text we have today.

Others determined that the books Deuteronomy to 2 Kings formed a single work that tells how the Israelites were exiled because they had been unfaithful to God's covenant.

On the whole, redaction criticism has helped us understand the theology of the biblical writers and has increased our knowledge of the history of Judaism and early Christianity.

113

Biblical Criticism Up to Now

THE VARIOUS WAYS IN WHICH WE READ SCRIPTURE

In the first half of the twentieth century, biblical scholars used the techniques of historical criticism to focus on how the biblical books were written and revised until they attained the form in which they now appear. In the second half of the century, efforts were made to see how biblical books functioned as part of the entire biblical canon. In the last few decades the forms of biblical criticism have increased dramatically, ranging from the simple to the highly complex.

Archbishop Oscar Romero of San Salvador put liberation theology into practice by preaching against the oppression of his people by their totalitarian government. He was assassinated in 1980 while celebrating Mass.

This painting by Domenico Morelli (1826–1901) depicts the lovers in the Song of Solomon, which has undergone at least three major types of study. Histories of how the Song of Solomon was interpreted by Jewish rabbis, fathers of the church, medieval monks, and even modern church leaders show that most regarded the book as an allegory of God's love for Israel or Jesus' love for the church. Literary studies of the book, however, see it as a love poem that closely resembles other ancient Near Eastern love songs. Feminist critic Phyllis Trible considers the Song of Solomon to be a response to the story of Adam and Eve, which she sees as a love story between equals gone wrong – while the Song of Solomon, with its ideal couple, redeems that love story.

THE HISTORICAL JESUS

Since the era of the Enlightenment scholars have been trying to discover the "historical" Jesus (Jesus as he was in real life) in the belief that the Jesus described in the Gospels is coloured by the theological views of the early church. In 1853 David Friedrich Strauss held that it was impossible to construct a historically accurate biography of Jesus, but countless theologians have subsequently tried. Using the techniques of historical criticism, writers have variously depicted Jesus as a cynic, a wandering preacher who shocked people into fresh thought about themselves, a non-political figure, a political figure, and a Jew who overcame the stigma of an illegitimate birth to become a rabbi and a mystic.

Meanwhile, the Jesus Seminar, a group of prominent American scholars, have been meeting to discuss the historicity of Jesus' sayings. Using a set of guidelines to help them, these scholars discuss, debate, and vote on the authenticity of Jesus' sayings according to a scale of probability. In the end, the diversity of opinions about the historical Jesus goes further in reflecting the personalities of these scholars than it shows what Jesus was really like.

We shall come much closer to the range of intended meanings – theological, psychological, moral, or whatever – of the biblical tale by understanding precisely how it is told.

ROBERT ALTER, *THE ART OF BIBLICAL NARRATIVE*

Types of Biblical Criticism

So many forms of biblical criticism have been employed in recent times that the terms can become confusing. Following is a list of the chief forms of biblical interpretation in use today, together with the focus of each:

■ *Textual criticism* sorts through ancient versions of the Bible to establish the most accurate text.

■ *Source criticism* traces oral or written sources used by the biblical authors.

■ *Form criticism* examines the literary forms that make up the Bible.

■ *Redaction criticism* looks at the work of the original authors and editors of the Bible to better understand their viewpoints.

■ *Canonical criticism* examines the ways in which texts function as part of the entire Bible.

■ *Interpretation history* studies biblical interpretations through the centuries to help us better understand the Bible today.

■ *Literary criticism* studies the Bible text on its own, within its literary genre and structure, not taking into consideration the historical context or the intentions of the author.

■ *Liberation theology* is used by people to interpret the Bible within the context of the situation of those around them, especially the poor and the oppressed.

■ *Feminist interpretation* examines how women are represented or misrepresented in the books of the Bible. It sometimes criticizes the biblical writers for being male-centred and covering up the true status of women in biblical times.

■ *Science-driven studies* have been undertaken to interpret the Bible. Sociologists have shown how a loose confederation of 12 tribes might have become a nation bound by a common religion. Anthropologists have shed light on the Old Testament ideas of kinship. Psychoanalysts have investigated the meanings of symbols.

■ *Fundamentalist interpretation* focuses on the verbal inerrancy of Scripture.

Naomi entreats her daughters-in-law Ruth and Orpah to remain in their homelands, as shown in this 1795 illustration by William Blake, but Ruth follows Naomi to Israel. Feminists have seen Ruth and Naomi as valiant women and have contrasted the idealized account of their story with the sombre accounts of victimized women, such as Jephthah's daughter, who was sacrificed by her own father (Judges 11:30–40).

The Bible and Literature

REIMAGINED VERSIONS OF BIBLICAL TEXTS

Almost from the beginning, the Bible has inspired literary masterpieces. In the early Middle Ages, Latin poems based on Bible stories were common. But by the seventh century, poems in the peoples' languages began to appear. Since most Christians could not read Latin (the language in which Bibles were rendered), poetry helped spread the message of God's word. Later poets and novelists used the Bible to retell stories and define characters by referring to their use or misuse of Scripture or by criticizing various points of view.

Early Poetry

Almost as soon as literature began to be written in Old English (Anglo-Saxon), poems inspired by the Bible appeared. The earliest was probably a hymn exalting God's creation by Caedmon, an illiterate herdsman of the seventh century.

Poems were also inspired by sacred objects. In about 1175, the French poet Chrétien de Troyes wrote *Perceval*, a poem about King Arthur's knights of the Round Table and their search for the holy grail – the cup from which Jesus drank. In the end Perceval is rewarded with sight of the grail because his heart is pure.

The first masterpiece of the Renaissance was the Italian poet Dante Alighieri's *Divine Comedy*, which was completed by 1321. In this three-volume epic, the poet is given a tour of hell, purgatory, and heaven. The work is filled with allusions to the Bible, and characters from the Bible appear in all three books. For example, in the *Inferno*, Dante shows Judas locked in the jaws of Satan at the frozen bottom of hell.

Comic poems also used the Bible. In *The Canterbury Tales*, written by the English poet Geoffrey Chaucer in the late fourteenth century, the wife of Bath banters on about the Samaritan woman in chapter 4 of John's Gospel to justify her own many marriages.

In *Paradise Lost*, the English Puritan poet John Milton created an epic poem by mixing the story of Adam and Eve in Genesis with the story of the fall of Lucifer from 1 Enoch.

Romantic and Nineteenth-Century Literature

The Romantic poets sometimes used the Bible to bolster their own views. For example, the English poet William Blake mixed mythological and biblical language to depict a universe of opposites, such as heaven and hell, good and evil, innocence and experience. "The Tyger", a poem in *Songs of Experience* (1794), is his meditation on God as creator.

American novelist Herman Melville offers a rich synthesis of biblical narrative

In about 1210 German poet Wolfram von Eschenbach wrote the epic poem *Parzival*, his own version of Chrétien de Troyes' *Perceval*. Centuries later Richard Wagner turned Eschenbach's epic into an opera. The hero is depicted here by Franz Stassen.

> *In the scriptures themselves, these plays upon words are to be found as well as in the best works of the ancients and in the most delightful parts of Shakespeare.*
>
> SAMUEL COLERIDGE, ENGLISH POET AND CRITIC

This nineteenth-century engraving by Gustave Doré shows Dante and Virgil crossing the River Styx, as described in Dante's *Inferno*.

Twentieth- and Twenty-First-Century Literature

The Irish expatriate James Joyce evokes the book of Revelation in his last novel, *Finnegans Wake* (1939). In "The Joking Jesus", his satirical poem, Jesus jocularly urges his followers to write down all he did, adding, "And tell Tom, Dick and Harry I rose from the dead."

T.S. Eliot, the American-born English poet, often drew from the Bible. "Journey of the Magi" (1927) focuses on the arduous journey the wise men make to visit the newborn Jesus. "A Song of Simeon" (1928) is a reflection on the song sung by the elderly prophet Simeon on finally seeing the Messiah.

The tetralogy *Joseph and His Brothers* (1933–43) by the German novelist Thomas Mann is an elaborate rewriting of Genesis. In Mann's elaboration of the biblical tales, the pharaoh Joseph serves is Akhenaton, noted for worshipping only one god – the sun disc Aton. Mann suggests a connection between Akhenaton's religious practices and the emerging monotheism of the Israelites. He also ties the stories to both past and future. For example, he connects Joseph's reappearance after being thought dead with both Christ's resurrection and the mythic resurrection of the Egyptian god Osiris.

In *Cry the Beloved Country* (1948) South African author Alan Paton fused the stories of the prodigal son and David and Absalom in a plea for compassion in his country. Australia's Patrick White often used biblical symbolism in his novels, and the title character in *Voss* (1957) is gradually revealed as a Christ figure.

In his 1950 novel *Barabbas*, Sweden's Pär Fabian Lagerkvist imagined what life was like for the criminal who was freed in the place of Jesus. John Steinbeck's *East of Eden* (1952) is a reworking of the story of Cain and Abel, set in twentieth-century California.

More recently, two unlikely authors turned to the Bible for material. Portuguese novelist José Saramago, an atheist, wrote *The Gospel According to Jesus Christ* (1991), which depicts Jesus as flawed and doubt-ridden, and *Cain* (2009), a sardonic diatribe delivered by the first fratricide, who sees God as a petulant, small-minded tyrant. Adopting a more traditional point of view, Anne Rice, an American noted for sensual novels about vampires, wrote *Christ the Lord: Out of Egypt* (2005) and *Christ the Lord: The Road to Cana* (2008), depicting the young Jesus in a family setting.

in *Moby Dick* (1851), a novel about a mad sea captain, Ahab, named after the king of Israel who opposed the prophet Elijah. The novel's narrator, named after Abraham's exiled son, opens the novel by stating, "Call me Ishmael." After hearing a sermon about Jonah, Ishmael is warned by a madman, named Elijah, not to sail with Ahab. When the expedition ends in disaster, Ishmael is the only survivor. The final superscription is from Job: "And I only am escaped alone to tell thee."

Russian novelist Fyodor Dostoyevsky portrayed a number of his fictional characters as Christ figures, including Myshkin in *The Idiot* (1868–69) and Alyosha in *The Brothers Karamazov* (1880). In *Les Misérables*, French writer Victor Hugo also created Christ figures in the bishop of Digne and – once converted – the hero Jean Valjean.

The Bible on Stage and Screen

FROM MEDIEVAL PLAYS TO TODAY'S MOVIES

Early Christian leaders condemned the theatre because Roman plays were often lewd, crude, and laced with profanity. Plays also glorified murder, adultery, and other kinds of immorality. Consequently, Christians stayed away, and for centuries plays were kept out of and away from the churches. But by the tenth century, theatre gradually began making its way into the churches, energizing the congregations. In the centuries since, Bible stories have been dramatized on stage, on television, and in movies worldwide.

Horse-drawn floats rolled by the audience, stopping at set places to act out scenes in their cycle of plays. As depicted in this lithograph by Kenneth Petts, the mystery of the nativity is being acted out.

Medieval Drama

Because church services were conducted in Latin, a language most Christians did not understand, congregations grew restless. So, in the late tenth century, the clergy began to act out short plays about events from the Bible to awaken interest in the liturgy. These dramatizations, though in Latin, became popular throughout Europe.

By the fourteenth century, members of trade guilds were performing longer plays in local languages on movable floats. In the course of a day, a series of plays would be performed at predetermined spots, beginning with the creation and proceeding through the Bible to Judgment Day. The guilds often chose subjects suited to their professions. For example, in York, shipbuilders staged a play about Noah and the ark.

It seems that by the late 1500s, biblical plays had run their course and secular plays had picked up the slack, including the plays of the great William Shakespeare.

Shakespeare and Beyond

Shakespeare's plays are filled with biblical language and biblical references. For example, in *The Merchant of Venice*, the Jewish villain Shylock refuses to dine with Christians because they eat pork, adding that Jesus drove the devil into a herd of pigs (Matthew 8:32).

In France Jean Racine wrote *Athalie* (1691), a tragedy centring on Athaliah, the Israelite princess who murdered her way to the throne of Judah (2 Kings 11:1–16). The Spanish playwright Pedro Calderón de la Barca, wrote plays focusing on the vanity and emptiness of life, reflecting Ecclesiastes.

The German poet Johann Wolfgang von Goethe drew heavily on the Bible for his two-part masterpiece, *Faust* (1808 and 1832), which tells of a medieval scholar who sells his soul to the devil. The play's "Prologue in Heaven" is taken from Job, and in the end Faust is saved by his wish to do good works and by the enduring love of a good woman, who combines the attributes of Jesus' mother Mary, and Mary Magdalene. In Part 1 Faust seeks consolation in translating the Bible into German.

More than a century later, American poet Archibald MacLeish's *JB* (1958) depicted Job as an American banker (JB for Job) who spars with God and the devil, while the Nigerian author Wole Soyinka's *The Swamp Dwellers* (1963) focuses on the prodigal son and the larger biblical theme of brothers in conflict. For the most part, though, biblical drama passed into the field of motion pictures and television.

A still from the 2014 blockbuster *Exodus* starring Christian Bale.

The Bible Goes to the Movies

In 1907 *Moses and the Exodus from Egypt*, a 10-minute French film, was released, beginning a trend that was still in progress in 2014, when Ridley Scott released *Exodus: Gods and Kings*, a longer and more elaborate version of the story. Possibly the most influential director of biblical epics was Cecil B. DeMille, who created two versions of *The Ten Commandments* (1923 and 1956), a life of Jesus called *The King of Kings* (1927), and a super-spectacular dramatization of *Samson and Delilah* (1949). Similar biblical epics were Henry King's *David and Bathsheba* (1951) and George Stevens' version of the Gospels, *The Greatest Story Ever Told* (1965). In 2000 Jeffrey Katzenberg produced an animated biblical film, *The Prince of Egypt* (2000).

In reaction to these Hollywood epics, the Italian director Pier Paolo Pasolini created a simple rendering of *The Gospel According to St Matthew* in 1964, while in 1988 Martin Scorsese stirred up controversy with *The Last Temptation of Christ* by showing Jesus being tempted to marry Mary Magdalene.

Biblical films have continued to be made in the twenty-first century. In Mel Gibson's *Passion of the Christ* (2004), realism is so stressed that the characters speak in Aramaic and Latin. In 2014, two biblical epics appeared: Ridley Scott's *Exodus* film and Darren Aronofsky's *Noah*, a lavish depiction of the flood story.

The Bible on Small Screens

Beginning in the 1960s, many biblical movies have been made for television. Most notable was Franco Zeffirelli's six-hour *Jesus of Nazareth* (1977), which has authentic settings and verbatim quotes from the Bible. In 2013 Roma Downey and Mark Burnett created the mini-series *The Bible*, which has been watched by more than 100 million people worldwide. The series was then turned into the feature film *Son of God* (2014). Another series, *The Bible*, includes "Genesis" (1994) in which an elderly desert nomad tells stories from Genesis, emulating ancient storytellers, and "Solomon", "Esther", and "Jeremiah" (all three released in 2000).

Greatest Adventure Stories from the Bible is a series of animated Bible stories, including "Noah's Ark", "Jonah", and "The Miracles of Jesus" (1993). There is also a British–Russian series entitled *Testament: The Bible in Animation*.

Other movies help explain the world of the Bible or how the Bible came to be. *Time Travel Through the Bible* (1990) and *Who Was Moses?* (2000) use archaeological finds and history to explore the world of the Bible. In 2011, the BBC produced a documentary to mark the 400th anniversary since the publication of the King James Bible called *The King James Bible: The Book That Changed The World*.

Recent European Texts

SCRIPTURE ON THE CONTINENT

As the world settled into a new millennium, the work of Bible translation was at an all-time high. New translations had appeared throughout Europe in the early twentieth century, and after the World Wars others were undertaken and completed. Often these new versions were made by interdenominational committees rather than individual missionaries. In all, according to the United Bible Societies, Bibles had been translated into 58 different European languages by 2014.

Renowned Jewish philosopher Martin Buber sought to give his German translation of Scripture the feel of the original Hebrew text. With the help of another philosopher, Gotthold Salomon, he produced a historic 15-volume translation of the Old Testament in 1925–37.

Recent Translations

Over the past 50 years, Europeans have produced dozens of new Bibles, ranging from translations into everyday language to multi-volume scholarly works. A few are listed below:

- **CZECH BIBLE:** A new Czech translation of the Bible was completed in 2009.

- **DANISH BIBLES:** In 2000 the Danes published Bibles in Danish, Faroese, and Greenlandic, using a matching format featuring designs created by Queen Margrethe II. It was felt that the uniform format showed that Denmark, the Faroe Islands, and Greenland form a spiritual community.

- **DUTCH BIBLES:** Today's Dutch Bible, an inter-confessional common language version, was completed in 1983 and revised in 1996. In October 2014 the *Bijbel in Gewone Taal*, the "Bible in Plain Language" was published.

- **FRENCH BIBLES:** Between 1974 and 1977, a 26-volume Bible appeared. Translated by André Nathan Chouraqui into Hebrew-flavoured French, it was the first French Bible translated by a Jewish scholar to include the New Testament. In 2000, the *Parole de Vie* was published by the French Bible Society, following the basic translation principles recommended by UNESCO. It uses only 3,000 words of vocabulary. In 2013 a new official liturgical Bible was published.

- **GERMAN BIBLES:** In 1980 the Bible was translated into German by a committee commissioned by Catholic bishops of Germany, Austria, Switzerland, Luxembourg, and Lüttich. Protestant scholars joined the committee to revise the New Testament.

- **ITALIAN BIBLES:** In 1968 Italy published the *Bibbia Concordata*, which was translated by a committee of Catholic, Protestant, and Jewish scholars. Another Italian version was made in 1971 by only three translators – to keep the text consistent. Held as Italy's official Catholic version of the Bible, it was totally redone in 2008 to take into account newly discovered documents for the New Testament.

● SEE ALSO
LUTHER AND HIS BIBLE, PP. 84–85
MORE REFORMATION-ERA BIBLES, PP. 86–87

A nation that receives the Bible in its own language will never be the same again.
MARTIN BUBER

■ **NORWEGIAN BIBLES:** The Bible was first translated into modern Norwegian in 1978 and revised in 1999. The newest translation, *Bible 2011*, was launched in 2011.

■ **POLISH BIBLES:** In 2001 a New Testament in Polish was published as part of a projected full Bible. The work is being done by a team of 30 scholars from Catholic, Orthodox, and Protestant traditions.

■ **RUSSIAN BIBLES:** Since the start of the millennium, the Bible Society of Russia has been translating Scripture into Russian and six other languages spoken in Russia. Greek–Russian and Hebrew–Russian interlinear Bibles and a critical edition of the Old Slavonic Gospels were also in the works.

■ **SPANISH BIBLES:** The first Bible to be translated into Spanish from the original languages was made in 1944. In 1992 a Spanish translation of the Bible based on the English New International Version was brought out.

■ **SWEDISH BIBLES:** In 1999 Sweden published *Bibel 2000*. This modern Swedish Bible was so successful that within weeks of publication, one in every ten people in Sweden had bought a copy.

■ **TURKISH BIBLES:** Although Turkey had produced a popular Bible in 1941, using the new Turkish alphabet instead of Arabic characters, young Turks were finding it difficult to understand. Consequently, a new translation was started in 1979. The New Testament was published in 1989, and the text was said to flow "like music". In 2001, the entire Bible appeared. In 2012 Jehovah's Witnesses published a complete Bible.

A Dutch version of Matthew's Gospel.

THE JERUSALEM BIBLE

Historically, the Catholic Church had been reluctant to approve translations of the Bible into the languages of the people. But this attitude changed in 1942, when Pope Pius XII issued an encyclical (official letter) calling for a more historic approach to biblical studies and for new and more accurate translations of the Bible.

The timing of the encyclical was ideal for Father Thomas Georges Chifflot, a Dominican priest and publisher in Nazi-occupied Paris. Father Chifflot had recently determined that the time had come for a new translation of the Bible, which would comfort, inspire, and instruct French Catholics. Encouraged by the pope's encyclical, he wrote to scholars at the École Biblique, a famous biblical studies institute in Jerusalem, asking them to undertake a translation based on the original Hebrew and Greek texts of the Bible and not on the Latin Vulgate that earlier Catholic translators had used. Because the Second World War was still raging, he got no response to his letter until 1945. Then, with the war ended, work on the translation began and progressed rapidly.

Preliminary translations of sections of the Bible were published between 1948 and 1954, and each was thoroughly revised (some more than once). Finally, a one-volume edition of the new translation was published in 1956 as the Jerusalem Bible. A revised version, based on later scholarly findings, was issued in 1973.

Not only was the translation of high calibre, but its scholarly notes, introductions and other extra features made the Jerusalem Bible invaluable. It served as a model for future study Bibles in German, Spanish, Vietnamese, Swahili, and the language of the Cree Indians of Ontario, Canada.

England produced a Jerusalem Bible in 1966 and revised it in 1985 to incorporate the changes made in the revised French version. Although the revised English version – the New Jerusalem Bible – relied more on the original Hebrew and Greek texts for its translations than on the French, it closely adopted the French introductions and notes, as did versions in other languages.

Pope Pius XII (1876–1958), who in 1942 signed a letter calling for more accurate translations of the Bible.

121

Specialized Bibles

SOMETHING FOR EVERYONE

There are more than just a few versions of the Bible. There are hundreds. And more are coming. Most printed Bibles have a unique slant or purpose. Many are theologically distinct, intended for evangelical Protestants, Catholics, Eastern Orthodox, or Jews. Others are written for people with different needs or interests: there are Bibles for students and Bibles for recovering addicts. There are also study Bibles, Bible encyclopedias, and highly illustrated luxury Bibles. The twenty-first century has also seen an enormous increase in digital products related to the Bible.

Devotional Bibles

Devotional Bibles are intended to help readers get the most out of their reflective time with the Bible. *The Inspirational Bible*, based on the New Century Version, offers short articles that sum up each passage and add inspiring thoughts and applications.

The *One-Year Bible* arranges passages into 15-minute readings designed to cover the entire Bible in a year.

Study Bibles

The typical study Bible presents the sacred texts in full, but adds explanatory notes that help modern readers understand ancient ways. For example, in the *HarperCollins Study Bible*, a marginal note is added for Matthew 3:7, explaining who the Pharisees mentioned in the text were. In the *Quest Study Bible* more than 6,000 questions a typical person might ask are answered in the margins. In contrast, *The Life Application Study Bible* is concerned with applying the Bible's message to the reader's life. *The Orthodox Study Bible* (2008) is the first full Orthodox study Bible in English and uses a new English translation of the Septuagint and extensive notes that centre on the Eastern commentators of the first millennium.

Churchgoers at Hope Community Church in Raleigh, North Carolina, use their smartphones to read the Bible during the sermon. Thousands have downloaded the church's app since its creation in 2012.

In another type of study Bible different versions of the sacred text are printed side by side in columns. And so the King James Version may appear with more modern translations or the original Greek text of the Gospels may be given next to an English translation. *The Synopsis of the Four Gospels* gives parallel translations of the Gospels to show where Matthew and Luke took from Mark and where they added material. Many of these products are available in print or e-book versions, on websites or as apps for phones, pads, and other devices.

Commentaries

Bible commentaries are basically advanced study Bibles – with more extensive and more scholarly notes. Some fast-paced commentaries cram all the notes into one or two volumes – generally without the biblical texts. Others are far more ambitious, such as the 12-volume *New Interpreter's Bible* (1994–99), which includes two translations of the biblical texts along with full commentaries for each book. For the more serious Bible students, there are separate commentaries for each book of the Bible. Complete sets of book-length commentaries range from classics, such as those of John Calvin (22 volumes) and Matthew Henry (6 volumes) to later collections, with different commentators for each book of the Bible.

The newer commentaries draw from the latest insights in archaeology, ancient languages, and scholarly discussion. The massive *Anchor Bible* presents new scholarly translations of each biblical book and adds exhaustive introductions, charts, maps, and textual and explanatory notes.

Reference Books

Supplementing the Bibles and commentaries are many other Bible-background books. Among the most common are encyclopedias, dictionaries, atlases, and concordances and topical Bibles, both of which help readers study a specific word or topic.

There are also books about Bible plants, animals, and people. There are books that focus on mysteries and tough questions in the Bible, such as how the parting of the Red Sea could have happened. And there are books that provide an overview of the Bible. For example, Stephen M. Miller's *Complete Guide to the*

● SEE ALSO
THE FIRST STUDY BIBLE, P. 47
BIBLES FOR KINGS AND NOBLES, PP. 68–69

Indeed, the word of God is living and active, sharper than any two-edged sword, piercing until it divides soul from spirit, joints from marrow; it is able to judge the thoughts and intentions of the heart.

HEBREWS 4:12

Bible (2008) is a lavishly illustrated guide that moves through the Bible book by book, offering background information, fascinating details of Bible times, and handy maps. Similarly, *The Lion Handbook to the Bible* (2009) features background information, maps, photos and explanations of chapters and events.

Finally, for those who prefer a more leisurely approach to getting immersed in the Bible, there are games. Among the many are: crossword puzzles, jigsaw puzzles, card games, and table games such as Bible Trivia and Bibleopoly, modelled on Monopoly.

The Bible in New Formats

Every kind of product mentioned so far is now available digitally. The rise of the Internet means that people are able to access the Bible wherever they go, either by visiting websites with Bible translations such as Bible Gateway, or by downloading Bible apps such as YouVersion.

Here are some of the most popular:

■ YouVersion is a Bible app that can be downloaded onto a phone, tablet, or computer free of charge. The user can read, listen, highlight, make notations, insert bookmarks, share with others, compare versions or languages, or watch Bible-related videos. On this and other apps users have access to a wide range of reading plans to guide them through daily readings of the Bible.

■ BibleGateway.com, a free website run by Zondervan designed to allow easy reading and searching of the Bible in 42 English versions and 47 different languages.

■ Study Bibles for tablets and smartphones in both modern and ancient languages, including dictionaries, glosses, and other study tools as well as Christian e-books for mobile, tablet, and desktop devices.

■ Logos Bible Software, a digital library app designed for Bible study that enables linking, note taking, and linguistic analysis of the Bible in translation or in its original languages.

■ Glo, another Bible app, utilizes HD video, photographs, maps, timelines, reading plans, and 360-degree virtual tours to enhance the experience of reading and understanding the Bible.

■ There is also a Bible app for kids (complete with cartoons).

The continuing growth of printed and electronic Bible products suggests that the best-selling book of all time will remain one of the best read and most intensely studied.

Jeffrey Smith, New Living Translation brand director at Tyndale House Publishers, poses with a stack of some of the different editions of the New Living Bible used in the YouVersion app, open on his iPad.

Sample views of the Glo Bible app.

Epilogue

Jesus' last words on earth explain why so many people throughout the ages have been willing to die for the sake of the Bible – to translate it, to teach it, and to live by its principles.

"Go into all the world and proclaim the good news to the whole creation," Jesus told his followers, moments before he ascended into the heavens. "You will be my witnesses in Jerusalem, in all Judea and Samaria, and to the ends of the earth" (Mark 16:15; Acts 1:8).

The eyewitnesses are gone. They died nearly 2,000 years ago. But their stories live on in the Bible, a book that Christians consider the only reliable testimony of God's good news about salvation.

From Genesis to Revelation – the Bible's first book to its last – Scripture follows God as he initiates and works his plan to eradicate sin from his once-perfect creation. God begins by calling a people, the Jews, to obey him and reap the rewards of his protection and blessing. This single nation is to serve as an example that will draw other nations to God, in the way light draws lost people at night. "All the nations of the earth shall gain blessing for themselves through your offspring," God promised Abraham (Genesis 26:4). About two millennia later, Jesus is born into a Jewish family. Proclaimed by angels as the Son of God, Jesus announces it is time to take God's message of salvation to everyone.

In a day yet to come, the New Testament promises, God's plan will be accomplished. "It is done!" God proclaims to John in an end-time vision of a creation where sin is gone:

> I am the Alpha and the Omega, the beginning and the end. To the thirsty I will give water as a gift from the spring of the water of life. Those who conquer will inherit these things, and I will be their God and they will be my children... and they will reign for ever and ever.

Revelation 21:6–7; 22:5

There are on this planet an estimated 6,500 languages. The Bible, complete or in part, is available in almost 2,900 languages. But the languages already translated are the major ones. Most of the others are regional dialects spoken by relatively few people. About nine out of ten people have at least some part of the Bible in their native language. Even so, many Christians are not satisfied. An estimated 600 Scripture translation projects are currently underway.

"Proclaim the good news to the whole creation," Jesus said.

> "Go into all the world and proclaim the good news to the whole creation."
> **Mark 16:15**

Index

Picture Acknowledgments

AKG Images: pp. 13t, 17 (woodcut, Julius Schnorr von Carolsfeld, 1860), 85b, 98t (oil on canvas, Andre Reinoso, 1619–22), 100t, 111t; p. 18bl Bible Land Pictures/Z. Radovan; p. 45 (marble, late 4th century) Erich Lessing; p. 53b (oil sketch, 1735–39) The National Gallery, London; p. 56t Mondadori Portfolio/Sergio Anelli; p. 64tr British Library; p. 73 Album/Oronoz; pp. 124–25 Stefan Diller

Alamy: p. 19 Hemis; p. 21t Jim Henderson; pp. 43b, 43t, 47t, 60t, 109r Bible Land Pictures; p. 46r The Art Archive; p. 56b Universal Images Group/DeAgostini; p. 58 WENN Ltd; p. 59 Peter Horree; p. 64l Kim Petersen; p. 83l Dennis Cox; p. 90b SuperStock; p. 94b age footstock; p. 96l (American lithograph) Niday Picture Library; p. 96r North Wind Picture Archives; p. 97m Everett Collection Historical; p. 104b GL Archive; p. 121l Stephen Barnes/Religion

Art Archive: p. 18t A. Dagli Orti; p. 20t (James Tissot) Jewish Museum, New York/Superstock; p. 44 (Italy, 4th century) DeA Picture Library/V. Pirozzi; p. 65 Bibliothèque Municipale Arras/Gianni Dagli Orti; pp. 67r, 70, 112 British Library; p. 78 (English school, late 16th century) Private Collection/Philip Mould; p. 88b Museo di Capodimonte, Naples/Dagli Orti; p. 92 (early 17th century) Museo del Prado Madrid/Dagli Orti

Beinecke Rare Book and Manuscript Library, Yale University: p. 48

Bridgeman Images: pp. 10l, 10r, 15b, 20b, 23t (this scroll dated to the 18th century), 25t, 28, 31 (*Landscape with St Philip Baptising the Eunuch*, Claude Lorrain, 1678), 36, 76, 77t (1517 portrait by Quentin Massys/Metsys), 81 (fresco, 1297–99), 84t, 87 (French school, 16th century), 94t (Mexican school, 18th century), 101b, 108l, 110 (*Noah's Ark*, Edward Hicks, 1846), 111b, 113, 114l, 115; pp. 9, 103t De Agostini Picture Library/A. Dagli Orti; p. 13b Christie's Images; pp. 14l, 27, 109t Zev Radovan; pp. 16 (depiction of Noah's ark, from a 12th-century version of *The Commentary on the Apocalypse* by Spanish monk Beatus of Liebana), 22 (Mesopotamian miniature from the 7th- to 8th-century Syriac Bible of Paris) Pictures from History; pp. 29b, 118 Look and Learn; p. 30 Tarker; pp. 32, 88t (Italian school, 17th century) Bonhams, London, UK; p. 71b The Board of Trinity College, Dublin, Ireland; p. 72 De Agostini Picture Library/G. Nimatallah; pp. 74, 82 British Library Board; p. 86t Universal History Archive/UIG; p. 89l Ken Welsh; p. 90t Stefano Baldini; p. 102b Corpus Christi College, Oxford, UK

Corbis: pp. 97tl, 97bl, 102t; p. 11t K.M. Westermann; p. 11m, 42t (detail from *Altarpiece of St Sebastian*, Pedro Garcia de Benabarre, 1455–56) Gianni Dagli Orti; p. 40 The Gallery Collection; p. 41 Alfredo Dagli Orti/The Art Archive; p. 42b *Martyrdom of Saint Ignatius of Antioch*, Giovanni Battista Crespi (1567/69–1632) Arte & Immagini srl; p. 46l Lowell Georgia; pp. 47b, 54 adoc-photos; p. 49r (11th-century fresco from a Cappadocian church) Chris Hellier; p. 51 Lynn Johnson/National Geographic Creative; p. 52 (fresco, Taddeo Gaddi (c. 1300–66)) Leemage; p. 60b Antoine Gyori/Sygma; p. 61 AMMAR AWAD/Reuters; p. 68 Elio Ciol; p. 97tr Lebrecht Authors/Lebrecht Music & Arts/Lebrecht Music & Arts; p. 108r Hulton-Deutsch Collection; p. 116 (scenography, for *Parsifal*, 1937) Alfredo Dagli Orti/The Art Archive

Getty: p. 21l Tish Wells/MCT; p. 25b Leemage; p. 29t Danita Delimont; pp. 35 (fresco dated 1305), 55b (*Jesus Stilling the Tempest*, 1886–94) SuperStock; pp. 50, 98b DeAgostini; p. 53 Mauro Magliani/Electa/Mondadori Portfolio; p. 55t Julian Love; p. 63 De Agostini/W. Buss; p. 69 The Print Collector; p. 77b PHAS; p. 80l ZU_09; p. 80r Culture Club; pp. 85t, 86b Universal History Archive; p. 114r Alex Bowie; p. 117 Prisma/UIG; p. 120 Universal History Archive/UIG; p. 122 Raleigh News & Observer; p. 123b Chicago Tribune

Kobal Collection: p. 119 20th Century Fox/Scott Free Productions

Mary Evans Picture Library: p. 106

Sonia Halliday: pp. 11r, 12, 14r, 26, 34, 38–39, 67l , 75t, 100b

Topfoto pp. 79, 101t; pp. 8t, 8b, 49l (1st century BC), 71t (portait by Francisco de Zurbarán, 1626–27), 83l World History Archive; pp. 15t, 37, 93 British Library Board; pp. 23b, 24 (Germany, 19th century), 62, 91, 95 (steel engraving, 1856), 99 (American engraving, 1837) The Granger Collection; p. 57 (dated 1460) HIP; pp. 66 (from the 12th-century Lambeth Bible), 103b Topham Picturepoint; p. 75b Nano Calvo; p. 84b Fine Art Images/HIP; pp. 89r, 121r Roger-Viollet

Wycliffe Bible Translators: pp. 104t, 105b, 105t

LION HUDSON

Commissioning editor: Becki Bradshaw
Project editor: Miranda Lever
Proofreader: Rachel Ashley-Pain
Book designer: Jonathan Roberts
Picture researcher: Jessica Scott
Production manager: Kylie Ord

54